THE REED OF GOD

Lignum habet spem:
si praecisum fuerit, rursum virescit,
et rami euis pullulant.

Job 14:7

Wood hath hope,
If it be cut, it groweth green again,
and the boughs thereof sprout.

CARYLL HOUSELANDER

THE REED OF GOD

Christian Classics, Inc.

WESTMINSTER, MARYLAND 21157

1987

Copyright © 1944 by Caryll Houselander

Eighth British edition, published by Sheed and Ward, Ltd.,
London, 1976

Nihil obstat: Patrick Morris, *Censor*
Imprimatur: E. Morrogh Bernard, *Vicar General*
    Westminster, April 13, 1944

Printed in the United States of America

Library of Congress Catalog Card No.: 78-51561
ISBN: 0-88479-013-4

TO DAVID AND ARCHIE

"Rhetoric's many followers were mute as fish when they saw Thee, O Mother of God; for they dared not ask: How canst thou bear a child and yet remain a Virgin? But we marvel at this mystery, and with faith cry:

Hail, vessel of the wisdom of God; hail, treasury of his foreknowledge.

Hail, thou that showest philosophers fools: hail, thou that provest logicians illogical.

Hail, for the subtle disputants are confounded; hail, for the writers of the myths are withered.

Hail, thou who didst break the webs of the Athenians; hail, thou who didst fill the nets of the fishermen.

Hail, thou who drawest us from the depths of ignorance; hail, thou who enlightenest many with knowledge.

Hail, raft for those who desire to be saved; hail, haven for those who swim on the waves of the world.

Hail, thou bride unwedded."

(THE AKATHIST HYMN)

CONTENTS

INTRODUCTION

When I was a small child someone for whom I had a great respect told me never to do anything that Our Lady would not do; for, she said, if I did, the angels in heaven would blush.

For a short time this advice "took" in me like an inoculation, causing a positive paralysis of piety.

It was clear to me that all those things which spelt joy to me were from henceforward taboo—blacking my face with burnt cork, turning somersaults between props against the garden wall, putting two bull's-eyes into my mouth at the same time—all that was over ! But even if I faced a blank future shackled with respectability, it was still impossible to imagine Our Lady doing anything that I would do, for the very simple reason that I simply could not imagine her doing *anything at all*.

The inoculation of piety wore off quickly, and so completely that when the sunset warmed the sky over our tangled garden with a pink glow, I thought that it must be the faint reflection of the rosy blush that suffused all heaven !

This would not be worth recording but for one thing, namely, that the wrong conception of Our Lady which I had is one that a great many other people have, too; a very great many people still think of Our Lady as someone who would never do anything that we do.

To many she is the Madonna of the Christmas card, immobile, seated forever in the immaculately clean stable of golden straw and shining snow. She is not real; nothing about her is real, not even the stable in which Love was born.

There are two things to-day which make it difficult for many people to love Our Lady.

First that she is pure and virgin. There is nothing so little appreciated by the world to-day as purity, nothing so misunderstood as virginity.

In many minds virginity is associated only with negative qualities, with impotence—impotence of body and mind, emotional and spiritual impotence.

Unfortunately, there are not only wise virgins in this world but unwise ones, foolish virgins; and the foolish virgins make more noise in the world than the wise, giving a false impression of virginity by their loveless and joyless attitude to life. They cause us to turn with a sigh of relief to the page in the Missal which announces the splendid feast of a holy woman who was neither a virgin nor a martyr.

These foolish virgins, like their prototypes, have no oil in their lamps. And no one can give them this oil, for it is the potency of life, the will and the capacity to love.

We no longer think of virginity as the first-fruits laid upon the fire of sacrifice, but rather as a windfall of green apples, which are hard and sour because the sun has never penetrated them and warmed them at the core.

Virginity is really the whole offering of soul and body to be consumed in the fire of love and changed into the flame of its glory.

The virginity of Our Lady is the wholeness of Love through which our own humanity has become the bride of the Spirit of Life.

It is this very fact which refutes the other mistaken idea about Our Lady, namely, that she is not human.

When we are attracted to a particular saint it is usually the little human details which attract us. These touches bridge the immense gap between heroic virtue and our weakness. We love most those saints who before they were great saints were great sinners.

But even those who were saints from the cradle are brought closer to us by recorded trifles of their humanness. How dear to us St. Catherine of Sienna is, because she loved her garden, because she made up little verses and gilded tiny oranges to humour a difficult Pope. How close she comes to us in her friendships: in the motley company of poets, politicians, soldiers, priests, and brigands—men who idolized her; and not only men, for St. Catherine was not only the most dynamic woman in history but also the best friend to other women that ever lived. Such things almost make us forget that she was fiercely ascetic, that for years she was fed only on the Blessed Sacrament, and that she was an ecstatic: her agony for the world's sin is hidden under the beautiful cloak of her love for sinners.

Of Our Lady such things are not recorded. We complain that so little is recorded of her personality, so few of her words, so few deeds, that we can form no picture of her, and there is nothing that we can lay hold of to imitate.

But it is Our Lady—and no other saint—whom we *can* really imitate.

All the canonized saints had special vocations, and special gifts for their fulfilment: presumption for me to think of imitating St. Catherine or St. Paul or St. Joan if I have not their unique character and intellect—which indeed I have not.

Each saint has his special work: one person's work. But Our Lady had to include in her vocation, in her life's work, the essential thing that was to be hidden in every other vocation, in every life.

She is not only human; she is humanity.

The one thing that she did and does is the one thing that we all have to do, namely, to bear Christ into the world.

Christ must be born from every soul, formed in every life. If we had a picture of Our Lady's personality we might be dazzled into thinking that only one sort of person could form Christ in himself, and we should miss the meaning of our own being.

Nothing but things essential *for us* are revealed to us about the Mother of God: the fact that she was wed to the Holy Spirit and bore Christ into the world.

Our crowning joy is that she did this as a lay person and through the ordinary daily life that we all live; through natural love made supernatural, as the water at Cana was, at her request, turned into wine.

In the world as it is, torn with agonies and dissensions, we need some direction for our souls which is never away from us; which, without enslaving us or narrowing our vision, enters into every detail of our life. Everyone longs for some such inward rule, a universal rule as big as the immeasurable law of love, yet as little as the narrowness of our daily routine. It must be so truly part of us all that it makes us all one, and yet to each one the secret of his own life with God.

To this need, the imitation of Our Lady is the answer; in contemplating her we find intimacy with God, the law which is the lovely yoke of the one irresistible love.

THE REED OF GOD

"As a clear and untilled space thou madest the divine ear of corn to burst forth; hail, thou living table having space for the Bread of Life; hail, perennial fountain of living water"

(THE AKATHIST HYMN)

EMPTINESS

THAT virginal quality which, for want of a better word, I call emptiness is the beginning of this contemplation.

It is not a formless emptiness, a void without meaning; on the contrary it has a shape, a form given to it by the purpose for which it is intended.

It is emptiness like the hollow in the reed, the narrow riftless emptiness which can have only one destiny: to receive the piper's breath and to utter the song that is in his heart.

It is emptiness like the hollow in the cup, shaped to receive water or wine.

It is emptiness like that of the bird's nest, built in a round warm ring to receive the little bird.

The pre-Advent emptiness of Our Lady's purposeful virginity was indeed like those three things.

She was a reed through which the Eternal Love was to be piped as a shepherd's song.

She was the flowerlike chalice into which the purest water of humanity was to be poured, mingled with wine, changed to the crimson blood of love, and lifted up in sacrifice.

She was the warm nest rounded to the shape of humanity to receive the Divine Little Bird.

Emptiness is a very common complaint in our days, not the purposeful emptiness of the virginal heart and mind but a void, meaningless, unhappy condition.

Strangely enough, those who complain the loudest of the emptiness of their lives are usually people whose lives are overcrowded, filled with trivial details, plans, desires, ambitions, unsatisfied cravings for passing pleasures, doubts, anxieties and fears; and these sometimes further overlaid with exhausting pleasures which are an attempt, and always a futile attempt, to forget how pointless such people's lives are. Those who complain in these circumstances of the emptiness of their lives are usually afraid to allow space or silence or pause in their lives. They dread space, for they want material things crowded together, so that there will always be something to lean on for support. They dread silence, because they do not want to hear their own pulses beating out the seconds of their life, and to know that each beat is another knock on the door of death. Death seems to them to be only the final void, the darkest, loneliest emptiness.

They have no sense of being related to any abiding beauty, to any indestructible life: they are afraid to be alone with their unrelated hearts.

Such emptiness is very different from that still, shadowless ring of light round which our being is circled, making a shape which in itself is an absolute promise of fulfilment.

The question which most people will ask is: "Can someone whose life is already cluttered up with trivial things get back to this virginal emptiness?"

Of course he can; if a bird's nest has been filled with broken glass and rubbish, it can be emptied.

It is not only trivialities which destroy this virgin-mindedness; very often, serious people with a conscious purpose in life destroy it by being too set on this purpose. The core of emptiness is not filled by trifles but by a hard block, tightly wedged in. They have a plan, for example, for reconstructing Europe, for reforming education, for converting the world; and this plan, this enthusiasm, has become so important in their minds that there is neither room to receive God nor silence to hear His voice, even though He comes as light and little as a Communion wafer and speaks as soft as a zephyr of wind tapping on the window with a flower.

Zealots and triflers and all besides who have crowded the emptiness out of their minds and the silence out of their souls can restore it. At least, they can allow God to restore it and ask Him to do so.

The whole process of contemplation through imitation of Our Lady can be gone through, in the first place, with just that simple purpose of regaining the virgin-mind, and as we go on in the attempt we shall find that over and over again there is a new emptying process; it is a thing which has to be done in contemplation as often as the earth has to be sifted and the field ploughed for seed.

At the beginning it will be necessary for each individual to discard deliberately all the trifling unnecessary things in his life, all the hard blocks and congestions; not necessarily to discard all his interests for ever, but at least once to stop still, and having prayed for courage, to visualise himself without all the extras, escapes, and interests other than Love in his life: to see ourselves as if we had just come from God's hand and had gathered nothing to ourselves yet, to discover just what shape *is* the virginal emptiness of our own being, and of what material we are made.

We need to be reminded that every second of our survival does really mean that we are new from God's fingers, so that it requires no more than the miracle which we never notice to restore to us our virgin-heart at any moment we like to choose.

Our own effort will consist in sifting and sorting out everything that is not essential and that fills up space and silence in us and in discovering what sort of shape this emptiness in us, is. From this we shall learn what sort of purpose God has for us. In what way are we to fulfil the work of giving Christ life in us?

Are we reed pipes? Is He waiting to live lyrically through us?

Are we chalices? Does He ask to be sacrificed in us?

Are we nests? Does He desire of us a warm, sweet abiding in domestic life at home?

These are only some of the possible forms of virginity; each person may find some quite different form, his own secret.

I mention those three because they are all fulfilled in Our Lady, so visibly that we may be sure that we can look at them in her and learn what she reveals through them.

It is the purpose for which something is made that decides the material which is used.

The chalice is made of pure gold because it must contain the Blood of Christ.

The bird's nest is made of scraps of soft down, leaves and feathers and twigs, because it must be a strong warm home for the young birds.

When human creatures make things, their instinct is to use not only the material that is most suitable from the point of view of utility but also the material most fitting to express the conception of the object they have in mind.

It is possible to make a candle with very little wax and a lot of fat, but a candle made from pure wax is more useful and more fitting; the Church insists that the candles on the Altar be made of pure wax, the wax of the soft, dark bees. It is beautiful, natural material; it reminds us of the days of warm sun, the droning of the bees, the summer in flower. The tender ivory colour has its own unique beauty and a kind of affinity with the whiteness of linen and of unleavened bread. In every way it is fitting material to bear a light, and by light it is made yet more lovely.

The purpose for which human beings are made is told to us briefly in the catechism. It is to know, love, and serve God in this world and to be happy with Him for ever in the next.

This knowing, loving, and serving is far more intimate than that rather cold little sentence reveals to us.

The material which God has found apt for it is human nature: blood, flesh, bone, salt, water, will, intellect.

It is impossible to say too often or too strongly that human nature, body and soul together, is the material for God's will in us.

There are many people in the world who cultivate a curious state which they call "the spiritual life." They often complain that they have very little time to devote to the "spiritual life." The only time that they do not regard as wasted is the time they can devote to pious exercises: praying, reading, meditations, and visiting the church.

All the time spent in earning a living, cleaning the home, caring for the children, making and mending clothes, cooking, and all the other manifold duties and responsibilities, is regarded as wasted.

Yet it is really through ordinary human life and the things of every hour of every day that union with God comes about.

Although human nature is the material which God has made for the fulfilling of His will in us, and although human nature is something we all share, and although we each have the same purpose of knowing and loving God, we do not all achieve that purpose in the same way or through the same experiences; in fact no two people have exactly the same personal experience of God; there seem to be rules of love like the rules of music, but within them each soul has her secret—with God.

Every person living is—besides being one of the human race—*himself*; and in order to make the raw material of *himself* what it *is*, innumerable different experiences and different influences have been used.

Here are some of the things which go towards making each human person what he is:

Heredity, environment, infant and child experience, opportunity, education or lack of education, friends or lack of friends, and the countless unpredictable things that we misname accidents or chance.

We are often reminded that we have been chosen by God out of innumerable potential people whom He did not create. But very seldom do we think about the mystery of all the years and all the people and all the gathered memories, both of individuals and races, which have made us individually what we are.

Our life has been given to us from generation to generation, existing in each age in the keeping of other human beings, tended in the Creator's hands, a little flame carried through darkness and storm, burning palely in brilliant sunlight, shining out like a star in darkness, life in the brave keeping of love given from age to age in a kiss.

To some these ages of experience and memory have handed down gifts of health and sound nerves and a buoyant attitude to life; to others gifts of mind, talents, sensitivity. Some are endowed with a natural Christianity; others inherit dark and terrible impulses and crumbling weakness, fears, and neuroses.

It is a great mistake to suppose that those who have inherited the material for their life from suffering generations, and who have poor health and a timid approach or some vice or weakness, have not been designed and planned by God as much as others who seem luckier in the world's eyes.

Christ has said: "I am the Way," and He has been there in every generation, blowing with the Divine Breath of the Spirit on that little flame of life. He is the Way, but He is not limited as we are: He can manifest Himself in countless ways we do not dream of. He can will to live in lives of suffering and darkness we cannot conceive of; He can choose what seems to us the most unlikely material in the world to use for a positive miracle of His love.

The tendency of our generation is to worship physical and material happiness, to set up types for the multitudes to emulate—hearty, healthy, insensitive types they are, as a rule, too; always young, usually aggressive.

These types are symbolic of the materialism of our age. They suggest a carefully camouflaged inferiority among the older people; for it is old people, frightened old people, who have set up this rather aggressive type. It is they who, in shelving their own responsibilities, their great obligation to be born again, are hoodwinking youth.

Christ is not restricted to any type: the glory of God is not more manifest in a strapping young man or woman marching behind the banner of Christianity than in one of the slaughtered innocents of Jerusalem or in the repentant thief dying on the cross.

The most striking example of the material God can and does use to manifest His glory is Lazarus.

Lazarus was not even alive; he was dead, and according to his chief mourners, stinking; but Christ used him as the material for showing forth the glory of God in a way surpassed only by His own Resurrection. The moment of His own Resurrection was secret, a secret between His Heavenly Father and Himself. But the raising of Lazarus dazzled the world.

Each one of us—as we are at the moment when we first ask ourselves: "For what purpose do I exist?"—is the material which Christ Himself, through all the generations that have gone to our making, has fashioned for His purpose.

That which seems to us to be a crumbling point, a lack, a thorn in the flesh, is destined for God's glory as surely as the rotting bones of Lazarus, as surely as the radiance of Mary of Nazareth.

Our own experience, the experience of our ancestors and of all our race, has made us the material that we are. This material gives us the form of our life, the shape of our destiny.

Think again of the three symbols I have used for the virginal emptiness of Mary. These are each made from material which must undergo some experience to be made ready for its purpose.

The reed grows by the streams. It is the simplest of things, but it must be cut by the sharp knife, hollowed out, and the stops must be cut in it; it must be shaped and pierced before it can utter the shepherd's song. It is the narrowest emptiness in the world, but the little reed utters infinite music.

The chalice does not grow like the flower it resembles. It is made of gold; gold must be gathered from the water and the mud and hewn from the rock, it must be beaten by countless little blows that give the chalice of sacrifice its fitting beauty.

The twigs and fluff and leaves of the bird's nest are brought from all sorts of places, from wherever the brave careful mother alights, with fluttering but daring heart, to fetch them, from the distances and explorations that only the spread wings of love know. It is the shape of her breast that moulds the nest to its inviting roundness.

Thus it is with us—we may be formed by the knife, pared down, cut to the least, to the minimum of our own being; we may be marked indelibly by a succession of strokes, blows from the gold-beater's hammer; or we may be shaped for our destiny by the love and tender devotion of a devoted family.

These are but three examples. Each one can, when he has cleared out the rubble even for a day, look honestly at the material from which he is made, and ask the Holy Spirit to let It show him the way Christ wills to show Himself in his life.

Does He ask to be sung, to be uttered as the Word?

Does He ask to be sacrificed, to be lifted up and to draw all men to Him?

Does He ask to be fostered, swaddled, cherished, the little unfledged bird in the human heart?

How much can we do ourselves at this stage of contemplation? Not very much, for now, as always, most of it is done by God.

There is, however, one big thing we can do with God's help, that is, we can trust God's plan, we can put aside any quibbling or bitterness about ourselves and what we are.

We can accept and seize upon the fact that what we are at this moment, young or old, strong or weak, mild or passionate, beautiful or ugly, clever or stupid, is planned to be like that. Whatever we are gives form to the emptiness in us which can only be filled by God and which God is even now waiting to fill.

FIAT

THE church keeps the Feast of the Annunciation on the twenty-fifth of March. There is still a touch of austerity upon the earth, there is still a silver emptiness in the skies, but expectation of spring is already stirring the human heart, the bud is beginning to break on the tree, the promise of blossom has quickened the spirit of man.

This is the season when we celebrate the wedding of the Holy Spirit with humanity, the wedding of the Spirit of Wisdom and Love with the dust of the earth.

I think the most moving fact in the whole history of mankind is that wherever the Holy Spirit has desired to renew the face of the earth He has chosen to do so through communion with some humble little human creature.

In the instances we know of, it has not been to great or powerful people that the Spirit has come but to the little or the frightened, and we have seen them made new, and known that the subsequent flowering of their lives was nothing else but Christ given to them by that sweet impact.

It is always a love story, a culmination of love between the Spirit of Light and the Bride of the Spirit.

This is something which can happen to everyone now, but it could not have happened to anyone but for the *fiat* of the peasant girl in Nazareth whom the whole world calls Our Lady.

It is in Our Lady that God fell in love with Humanity.

It is upon her that the Dove descended, and the love of God for Humanity culminated in the conception of Christ in the human race.

When she surrendered herself to God, there was indeed a miraculous New Heaven and New Earth. The Spirit entered the world—light and wisdom and love, patience, fortitude, and joy entered the human heart and mind, and in the sight of God a springtime of loveliness woke in the world.

In the virginal emptiness of the girl, Mary of Nazareth, Christ was conceived; it was the wedding of God to a human child, and the wonder of it filled the earth for all time.

"He hath set His tabernacle in the sun: and He is as a bridegroom coming out of His bride chamber. His going out is from the end of heaven: and His circuit even to the end thereof" (Ps. xviii. Gradual of the Mass of Ember Saturday in Advent).

Christ's insistence on the power of children is very striking.

Almost more than anything else in the Gospel it proves that in God's eyes *being* something comes before *doing* something.

He sets a little child among his apostles as an example of what He loves. He says that heaven is full of children.

Indeed, the Architect of Love has built the door into heaven so low that no one but a small child can pass through it, unless, to get down to a child's little height, he goes in on his knees.

How consistent it is with the incredible tenderness of God that His Christ, the Immortal Child, should be conceived by the power of the Spirit in the body of a child. That a child should bear a Child, to redeem the world.

Our Lady was at the most fourteen when the angel came to her; perhaps she was younger.

The whole world trembled on the word of a child, on a child's consent.

To what was she asked to consent?

First of all, to the descent of the Holy Spirit, to surrender her littleness to the Infinite Love, and as a result to become the Mother of Christ.

It was so tremendous, yet so passive.

She was not asked to do anything herself, but to let something be done to her.

She was not asked to renounce anything, but to receive an incredible gift.

She was not asked to lead a special kind of life, to retire to the temple and live as a nun, to cultivate suitable virtues or claim special privileges.

She was simply to remain in the world, to go forward with her marriage to Joseph, to live the life of an artisan's wife, just what she had planned to do when she had no idea that anything out of the ordinary would ever happen to her.

It almost seemed as if God's becoming man and being born of a woman *were* ordinary.

The whole thing was to happen secretly. There was to be no announcement.

The psalmists had hymned Christ's coming on harps of gold. The prophets had foretold it with burning tongues. But now the loudest telling of His presence on earth was to be the heartbeat within the heartbeat of a child.

It was to be a secret and God was so jealous of His secret that He even guarded it at the cost of His little bride's seeming dishonour.

He allowed Joseph to misjudge her, at least for a time.

This proved that God knew Our Lady's trust in Him was absolutely without limit. Everything that He did to her in the future emphasized the same thing. His trust in her trust in Him.

The one thing that He did ask of her was the gift of her humanity. She was to give Him her body and soul unconditionally, and—what in this new light would have seemed absurdly trivial to anyone but the Child Bride of Wisdom—she was to give Him her daily life.

And outwardly it would not differ from the life she would have led if she had not been chosen to be the Bride of the Spirit and the Mother of God at all !

She was not even asked to live it alone with this God who was her own Being and whose Being was to be hers.

No, He asked for her ordinary life shared with Joseph. She was not to neglect her simple human tenderness, her love for an earthly man, because God was her unborn child.

On the contrary, the hands and feet, the heart, the waking, sleeping, and eating that were forming Christ were to form Him in service to Joseph.

Yes, it certainly seemed that God wanted to give the world the impression that it is ordinary for Him to be born of a human creature.

Well, that is a fact. God did mean it to be the ordinary thing, for it is His will that Christ shall be born in every human being's life and not, as a rule, through extraordinary things, but through the ordinary daily life and the human love that people give to one another.

Our Lady said yes.

She said yes for us all.

It was as if the human race were a little dark house, without light or air, locked and latched.

The wind of the Spirit had beaten on the door, rattled the windows, tapped on the dark glass with the tiny hands of flowers, flung golden seed against it, even, in hours of storm, lashed it with the boughs of a great tree—the prophecy of the Cross—and yet the Spirit was outside. But one day a girl opened the door, and the little house was swept pure and sweet by the wind. Seas of light swept through it, and the light remained in it; and in that little house a Child was born and the Child was God.

Our Lady said yes for the human race. Each one of us must echo that yes for our own lives.

We are all asked if we will surrender what we are, our humanity, our flesh and blood, to the Holy Spirit and allow Christ to fill the emptiness formed by the particular shape of our life.

The surrender that is asked of us includes complete and absolute trust; it must be like Our Lady's surrender, without condition and without reservation.

We shall not be asked to do more than the Mother of God; we shall not be asked to become extraordinary or set apart or to make a hard and fast rule of life or to compile a manual of mortifications or heroic resolutions; we shall not be asked to cultivate our souls like rare hothouse flowers; we shall not, most of us, even be allowed to do that.

What we shall be asked to give is our flesh and blood, our daily life—our thoughts, our service to one another, our affections and loves, our words, our intellect, our waking, working, and sleeping, our ordinary human joys and sorrows—to God.

To surrender all that we are, as we are, to the Spirit of Love in order that our lives may bear Christ into the world—that is what we shall be asked.

Our Lady has made this possible. Her *fiat* was for herself and for us, but if we want God's will to be completed in us as it is in her, we must echo her *fiat*.

This is not quite such an easy thing to do as it seems.

Most people, unless the invitation comes to them in early childhood, have already thrust down fierce roots into the heavy clay of the world. Their hands are already gripping hard on to self-interest. They are already partly paralysed by fear.

To put aside suddenly every motive except this single one, the forming of Christ in our life, is not so easy for ordinary people who are to remain ordinary.

The surrender we shall make will ask two hard things of us straight away.

The first of these hard things is that through being wed to the Spirit, we shall receive the gift of understanding.

In the world in which we live to-day, the great understanding given by the Spirit of Wisdom must involve us in a lot of suffering. We shall be obliged to see the wound that sin has inflicted on the people of the world. We shall have X-ray minds; we shall see through the bandages people have laid over the wounds that sin has dealt them; we shall see the Christ in others, and that vision will impose an obligation on us for as long as we live, the obligation of love; when we fail in it, we shall not be able to escape in excuses and distractions as we have done in the past; the failure will afflict us bitterly and always.

We shall have, by virtue of this same gift of understanding, far truer values; and we shall be haunted by a nostalgia for divine things, by a homesickness for God which is not eased in this world even by the presence of God.

And in proportion to our understanding we are likely to be misunderstood; the world does not accept Christ's values. The Beatitudes are madness to the world. "Blessed are the poor, the mourners, the reviled, the persecuted, the calumniated; blessed are those who hunger and thirst after Justice."

People who will not compromise with Christ's values are uncomfortable neighbours for mediocrity; they are likely to be misunderstood; they are often hated.

The world has set up a new set of Beatitudes. They run something like this: "Blessed are the comfortably well off, the cheerful, the highly respected. Blessed are the flattered. Blessed are those who are bored for a good salary on six days in the week and can overeat on the seventh. Blessed are those who are satisfied by the Beveridge plan and are always willing to compromise; blessed are they when all men respect their rights as citizens and forget that they are men, for their reward will not be very great but they will never be unduly disturbed and they will never disturb the complacency of others."

But if the misunderstanding of the world outside our homes can afflict us, it is nothing at all compared with the misunderstanding of those who are very dear to us (and this is so frequent that it is almost inevitable)— those whom we must love as Mary loved Joseph, that Christ may be formed in us from our very love for them. It is very often those people who are the most bewildered by the mystery of our surrender to the Holy Spirit.

Moreover, just as it was with Our Lady and St. Joseph, the tragedy of misunderstanding between us and our loved ones seems the more baffling because we both are convinced that our own point of view is right, our own actions the fulfilling of God's will.

The words, the actions that hurt us most, often torment those who utter them, just as Joseph must have torn and rent his own mind and heart when he questioned if it were God's will that he should put his young love from him.

Even when this is not so, it is still so natural that it is almost inevitable that those with whom our lives are interlocked should be hurt and frightened when our surrender first takes place, for it will almost certainly reverse all our values and theirs.

One newly converted to the Faith, or reawakened to its meaning, is one who has fallen in love with God, and everyone in the house will feel the presence, the danger of the Divine Lover, whose demands may be uncompromising, may turn the complacency of the middle way topsy-turvy; the presence of the Lover who, to the beloved newly aware of Him, will be utterly irresistible.

He is the Pied Piper to the human heart. He makes people become little children and suddenly turn the world they live in upside down, because they have been enchanted by Him.

Christ the invisible Piper in the home is just like the Catholic Church in the world; other religious, social, political organizations may arouse opposition, but the incurable disquiet of those who fear the Catholic Church is due to the fact that while all the others are systems, the Church is a Person, an incalculable Person, a Person with infinite power and a Child's values: the Person of Jesus Christ.

We know perfectly well that there are often scandals in the Church, that despite her pure heart, her children sometimes grow worldly and base and dress her up with tawdry golden garments which they have woven with black and cunning fingers; sometimes we see nothing but ugliness in her. Yet, even so, she is the refuge and hope of all sinners, the joy and hope of all saints, the life and hope of every living creature; and this is because under this aspect the Church is still Christ, Christ in His Passion, Christ crowned with thorns, His face covered in blood and dirt and the dust of the road on which we flung Him down. He still remains the one ultimately irresistible Person. This is why the Church is sometimes hated—"Wonder not if the world hate you"—sometimes feared; it is the mystery of utter love which is recognized, if not by the head, at least by the heart, and which no wounding and no disfiguring can hide. "He has no comeliness whereby we shall know Him." But we know Him without comeliness.

St. Peter walked on the stormy sea, but when his faith wavered he began to sink; and Christ rebuked him: "Oh thou of little faith, why didst thou doubt?"

What courage it would take to try to walk on the sea, even if we could see the face of Christ; but it needs much more courage to leave our false securities, our leaking boats of materialism, and to walk towards Him on the churned-up, angry sea of our civilization.

It would be a heroic thing to do even if we could see Him, but when the face of Christ is hidden in the darkness of our heart, then it requires all the heroism of Our Lady's *fiat*.

No wonder that those whose lives are locked into our own, to whom our wellbeing is their own wellbeing, are instinctively afraid of this *fiat*, which is so complete a disarming to God.

So completely have we depended upon material things, on money in particular, so terribly are we influenced by fear, that simply to abandon ourselves to God and really to mean it seems to be madness. Those who care for us see that we are in danger of becoming poor, as we really replace the old maxims such as: "Charity begins at home"; "It is my duty to look after myself"; "Business is business," and so on, by, "If a man asks for your coat, give him your cloak also"; "He who saves his life shall lose it"; and "Go sell what thou hast and give it to the poor."

"Be it done unto me according to thy word" seems a very bold prayer indeed in view of the words we know God has uttered. It would be easier to sacrifice some big thing to God, to impose some hard rule upon ourselves, than to say, "Do what you like with me."

For us poor creatures it is easier to trust someone who shares our insufficiency than to trust God, whose values are still past our comprehension. Those who love us see our new trust in God, but see with our own old blindness and mistrust. If God does not make us poor and disreputable and unworldly, He is (they think) at least certain to make us ridiculous.

The story of Joseph's bewilderment when he realized that his future wife was going to have a baby is well known, and it is well known, too, that Our Lady did not explain.

Her example here teaches us wisdom, when misunderstandings arise because of Christ conceived in us. There is little gained by trying to explain. At that time, the Advent time, His voice is silent in us; it is simply our own heartbeat. Love is more effective then than words.

The only thing to do is to go on loving, to be patient, to suffer the misunderstanding. Explanations even of what *can* be explained seldom heal—and there is so much that cannot be explained.

Even the presence of Christ in us does not do away with our own clumsiness, blindness, stupidity; indeed, sometimes because of *our* limitations, His light is a blinding light to us and we become, for a time, more dense than before. We shall still be irritable, still make mistakes, and still very likely be unaware of how exasperating we are.

Explanations, words, at this stage, may only wound, but love will be a bridge over which at last, in God's time, we shall cross to a better understanding.

It will have to be the love of humility, that is, love informed by humility—long-suffering, patient, and humorous. If we realize that we are a little absurd, such love will come more easily. We must try to be like Our Lady, to make as little fuss as she did about being the Mother of Christ.

No one can be so recollected, so tranquil, that he can be a contemplative in the world, a contemplative of Christ in his own heart, unless at the very outset he finds a cure for fear.

There is only one cure for fear—trust in God. That is why the beginning of Christ's being formed in us consists in echoing Our Lady's *fiat*; it is a surrender, a handing over of everything to God.

Many people feel that they could achieve heroic sanctity if they could do it in the way that appeals to them, for example, by being martyred. They can picture themselves going cheerfully to the stake; they can positively revel in being hanged, drawn, and quartered; but if

God makes no revelation but just lets them go on carrying out an insignificant job in the office day after day, or asks them to go on being gentle to a crotchety husband or to continue to be a conscientious housemaid, they are not willing. They do not trust God to know His own will for them.

Most people trust finite, helpless creatures more than they trust God, and this for the oddest of reasons—namely, that the finite, helpless creature is as frightened as they are; both are clinging to the same false securities.

We are afraid of birth, of life, of pain, of loss, of death.

All through our life we are dogged with fear. Some fears knit us together in sympathy, make us aware of our dependence upon one another.

We sense vaguely that we belong to one family, but not always that we have one Father, God.

We are afraid of birth, of the pain, the crudity, the fierceness of birth, of the responsibility of the new life.

We are afraid of life, of its continual demand on us, of its continual challenge to us: we are afraid of pain, of sickness, and of the pains and sickness of others.

Who does not know the hard anguish of waiting in the specialist's reception room for the verdict on some-one dear to us, the dreadful certainty of the verdicts of modern science, the blood-test and the X-ray?

And the fevers of little children: the bright blackness of the eyes, the mouths burning suddenly like malignant dark flowers, and the dreaded six o'clock, when we must look at the thermometer and we dare not look!

Who has not known fear of the death that comes slowly to old people, old people who are dear to us and who die, or seem to die, in little bits.

And who does not know the fear of loneliness and poverty in old age?

Then there is the daily, petty fear; fear of losing a hated job—a job that cramps and constricts the heart but which means the four walls of home, the food and warmth for the little family—fear that moves in a vicious circle, making us hate because we cringe and cringe because we hate.

We have had it instilled into us since we were in the cradle that the one security is money, money alone can save us. If we were a spiritually virile people, we should not worship money but should be grateful for it; it would simply be the symbol of work that satisfied us as men and women and provided the good bread, the warm wool, the fire in the hearth, and the sweetness of sleep in the home.

But we are not virile. We are weak, humiliated, dependent on bought things: drugs, anaesthetics, alcohol, distractions, escapes from ourselves, escapes from our humiliations. We are afraid for ourselves, but a thousand times more afraid for those we love.

When we love, the object of our love seems very frail. If he is at sea, how towering and black are the waves, how light, like an eggshell, the boat, and all night long, and all day long, the towering dark waters are beating against our frightened hearts.

How bitter the wind is when the object of our love is in the lash of it, and how pitiful his body, the visible shoulder blades, the ribs, how vulnerable they are and how sharp the wind, the east wind with its knife-cut of death!

And how great is the distance of a few miles when we are separated, how illimitable the sea.

Money means the safest, swiftest travelling, the speediest spoken or written word, the warmest clothing, the best medical aid.

Small wonder is it that gradually, without knowing it, we have come to trust more in money than in God.

From his earliest childhood the modern man is brought up to value money above all else and even to value himself by his capacity for getting it.

It is hardly surprising when we think of all that money has come to mean to men, that if the bread-winner suddenly changes his mind and sets some other thing higher, he is thought to be a traitor in his own home.

A boy is told that the object of his life is to "get somewhere," and that means to get money; that it is up to him to "make good," and that means to make money.

From his tenderest years he is submitted to nerve-racking tests of his potential money-making capacity. The school examinations have come to mean that; he must pass well because otherwise he will not get a good job, in other words, a job with a good salary.

Education is no longer primarily intended to teach him to serve God, or to enrich his life, but only to give him a passport into the commercial scramble.

Many sensitive boys break down under the strain of examinations, not because they are wanting in the knowledge necessary to pass, but because each one they do pass brings them a step nearer to the world of competition, in which, they know instinctively, so much that is fine in them will perish.

There are very big groups of society in which men value the esteem of their next-door neighbour more than their own self-esteem, and the next-door neighbour assesses them not by what they are but by what they have.

Poor, frightened little men, they depend for their courage to face the world on a little villa, overfurnished and packed with ornaments, a telephone, a radio, a small car, and a wife with a permanent wave.

Fed in this soil of vanity and fear and folly, the love for material things grows like a fungus in the soul and destroys the loveliness of the human heart utterly.

The remedy for fear is trust in God.

If we fear for ourselves or if we fear for others, it is all the same: trust in God is the only remedy.

Powerful to alleviate, to delay, to camouflage, though money is, in the end it lets us down.

Even when we have it we are continually anxious about losing it.

Even without the lesson of war, those who have lived long enough know that death finally defeats money, that there are dissensions and troubles between people that money cannot heal, and that at best the power it has is temporary and uncertain.

God is everlasting, certain, unchanging.

What is certain about Him is that He is love, that He loves both you and the person that you love, more than you do.

Your child is first of all God's child; your love for your little son is nothing, absolutely nothing at all, beside God's love for him.

Your little son is God's son; he is His only son, for Christ is in him, and God looks upon him and sees him as Christ, the one, only object of His Eternal love. He is the dearest of all creatures; he is the apple of God's eye.

When you watch him strutting round, showing off, troubling you, when you look at him in his sweetest moments and are moved to tenderness, when you see him excelling in games and lessons and are proud of him, you are not alone, far from it; God is watching him with the intent, absorbed love of a father for his only son.

When he is sick and you stand by the bedside shaken with fear, when he sleeps and you lean over him held by the amazement of seeing this little boy who has your life, God is there, too; indeed all this love of yours *is* only God's love which you sense vaguely. He, the true father, is there; He is around and above and below the child; He is in his heart. You only love at all because God loves infinitely more.

"Be it done unto me according to thy word" surrenders yourself and all that is dear to you to God, and the trust which it implies does not mean just trusting God to look after you and yours, to keep you and them in health and prosperity and honour.

It means much more, it means trusting that *whatever* God does with you and with yours is the act of an infinitely loving Father.

The war has shown even the inexperienced, the young, that you cannot depend on money. In less than a few seconds the richest man's home becomes a heap of rubble; at the same moment the little son is killed.

Is trust of God to go as far as that ? Are we to see the pathetic little burden carried away in the warden's arms and still say: "That is God's dear son, the object of all His all-powerful love!"

When Our Lady stood up, a queenly child, and uttered her *fiat* to the Angel of God, her words began to make Christ's voice. Those first words of consent had already spoken Christ's last words of consent; her "I commit myself to you, do whatever you like with me" were already spoken by Christ in her; they were one and the same with His: "Father, into thy hands I commend my spirit."

At that moment, when Our Lady received the love of the Holy Spirit as the wedded love of her soul, she also received her dead son in her arms. The trust which accepted the utter sweetness of the Infant Jesus between her own hands, looking at her with her own eyes, accepted the stiff, unresponsive corpse that her hands embalmed. This was her son, but more, even more, God's Son. She trusted God, she understood on earth that which many mothers will only understand in heaven; she was able to see her boy killed, lying there bruised from head to foot, wounded and dead, and to believe the Father's cry: "This is my beloved Son, in whom I am well pleased."

God asks for extreme courage in love; the Bride of the Spirit must respond with strength like His own strength.

Our Lady did this.

How much easier it would have been for her, had she been asked in that moment in time to withdraw from the common life, to tear up her heart by its roots and, renouncing all "earthly joys," bring forth Christ in cloistered security.

How much easier for her if she had had at least a guarantee for the safety of the precious burden, Christ, in her.

But she was consenting not only to bear her own child, Christ, but to bear Christ into the world in all men, in all lives, in all times; not only in secluded lives, protected lives, the lives of holy people, but into the lives of those haunted by worry, by poverty, by debts, by fears and temptations, subject to chance, to accident, to persecution, to the fortunes of war.

She was consenting not only to give birth to Christ, not only to give life to Him, but to give Him death.

In her brief historical life, of which we know so little, the history of the whole world is concentrated, particularly the lives of all the common people of the world, who often do not know themselves that they are Christ-bearers, living the life of the Mother of God.

She began at once, as she stood up before the angel and uttered her *fiat*, to live all our lives, and Christ in her was subject to the unknown, to the hazards of life in the world, as He is in us.

There are people who are afraid to suffer. There are others who are afraid not to suffer; it is true that they have not all got the truly magnificent spirit of St. Teresa of Avila with her cry: "Let me suffer or die"—they are not always by any means willing to suffer *any-thing* God wants of them; they prefer to choose, and sometimes one is wickedly tempted to smile at the choice.

As a small child I was very much inclined to give my mother my own favourite candies for her birthday, though *she* did not care for them. We are apt to treat God in this way, to offer Him the thing we shall enjoy ourselves. Again, our choice of suffering is sometimes so impossible for us to achieve that one wonders whether the luxury of *thinking* we want to suffer it is not the secret we are keeping from ourselves.

I knew once the primmest old invalid lady who could well have offered her helplessness to God, but she had a grievance with Him because He had not permitted her to be eaten by a cannibal for the Faith; she could not accept herself as a sick woman but she would have achieved heroic virtue as a cutlet!

There are some who are really afraid that they are unworthy of suffering at all, who do not realize the value of the rather *unfair* wear and tear of daily life. They feel forgotten and left out of God's plan.

The wonderful thing about Our Lady is that in her trust *everything* is included; she accepted her son as God's Son, she accepted His death without doubting God's love, her words were His words: "Be it done unto me according to thy word."

"Not my will but thy will be done."

She never changed or took back anything, she never made conditions with love.

But certainly at first there was nothing to suggest that being the Mother of God would involve her in anything more heroic than the joys and sorrows of her domestic life.

The sorrows of the whole world, not only the dramatic ones but the daily ones, began to unfold gradually in her life, and the intelligent heart can read into them not only the broad outline of all the world's tragedies but also the smallest details of human existence.

She did not feel slighted because there was not more in the beginning; she accepted the joy as readily as the sorrows of the world—her reconciliation with Joseph, the tenderness of his understanding when the angel had enlightened him, the pleasure of getting the house ready and making clothes for the coming child.

As to Joseph himself, now that he was one with her

as never before, he must have set about making a wooden cradle and have rejoiced that he had his trade in Nazareth and could look after Mary.

It must have been wonderful for him to see her at his table eating the food earned by the work of his hands and knowing that it nourished both her and the Messias; he must have looked at her often when she slept and felt his heart expand within his breast like a rose opening in a dark room, while he whispered the words of the scriptures, so familiar to him: "He giveth His beloved sleep."

But when he was in Bethlehem and Christ was born, one by one his troubles crowded in—the command not to return home, the hardships of the journey into Egypt and being obliged to see Mary and the Infant endure them, the struggle in the foreign country, starting again, trying to build up a trade, to learn the language.

Perhaps God sent the Magi with their gifts to Bethlehem that Joseph might sell the golden crowns to buy carpenter's tools in Egypt.

Looking about us now we can see all these things which were started and lived so intensely by those unknown peasants Joseph and Mary. We can see them happening all over the world, to everyone in the world. We can see that the human race, with its great vocation to be the Mother of God, is experiencing the very things that Mary and Joseph experienced when Christ was still a child in the womb.

A little while ago I went to register for National Service, Compulsory Registration. A group of women were waiting outside the doors for our turn; several carried babies in their arms; one was pregnant (we gave her the only chair); one of them grumbled: "No use for us to register," she said, "for in any case those with kiddies will have to stay at home."

I looked at the pregnant woman, and I thought of that great Registration at Bethlehem, when a poor peasant woman came in obedience; she need not have done so;

she could have claimed exemption. But Mary never claimed exemption from the common lot, from the circumstances that would be the common lot of all women for all time.

She knew it was "useful"—that those who are patient, obedient, humble, will be the mothers of Christ, will give *Life* back to the world.

"Be it done unto me . . ."

She spoke for all those poor women who stood with me waiting to register in the Second World War.

Everywhere the Flight into Egypt goes on: the little home is forsaken, the child in peril, the innocents slain; everywhere the refugees—Jesus, Mary and Joseph—come to us: strangers, foreigners in a strange land from every country in Europe—Czechoslovakia, Poland, Greece, Holland, France, Norway, Denmark, Malta, Gibraltar, Austria, Bavaria, Germany. For them all Our Lady has answered, long ago: "Be it done unto me."

In this great *fiat* of the little girl Mary, the strength and foundation of our life of contemplation is grounded, for it means absolute trust in God, trust which will not set us free from suffering but *will* set us free from anxiety, hesitation, and above all from the *fear* of suffering. Trust which makes us willing to be what God wants us to be, however great or however little that may prove. Trust which accepts God as illimitable Love.

ADVENT

ADVENT is the season of the seed: Christ loved this symbol of the seed.

The seed, He said, is the Word of God sown in the human heart.

"The Kingdom of Heaven is like to a grain of mustard seed."

"So is the Kingdom of God as if a man should cast seed into the earth."

Even his own life-blood: "Unless the grain of wheat falling into the ground die, itself remaineth alone."

The Advent, the seed of the world's life, was hidden in Our Lady.

Like the wheat seed in the earth, the seed of the Bread of Life was in her.

Like the golden harvest in the darkness of the earth, the Glory of God was shrined in her darkness.

Advent is the season of the secret, the secret of the growth of Christ, of Divine Love growing in silence.

It is the season of humility, silence, and growth.

For nine months Christ grew in His Mother's body. By His own will she formed Him from herself, from the simplicity of her daily life.

She had nothing to give Him but herself.

He asked for nothing else.

She gave Him herself.

Working, eating, sleeping, she was forming His body from hers. His flesh and blood. From her humanity she gave Him His humanity.

Walking in the streets of Nazareth to do her shopping, to visit her friends, she set His feet on the path of Jerusalem.

Washing, weaving, kneading, sweeping, her hands prepared His hands for the nails.

Every beat of her heart gave Him His heart to love with, His heart to be broken by love.

All her experience of the world about her was gathered to Christ growing in her.

Looking upon the flowers, she gave Him human sight. Talking with her neighbours, she gave Him a human voice. The voice we still hear in the silence of souls saying: "Consider the lilies of the field."

Sleeping in her still room, she gave Him the sleep of the child in the cradle, the sleep of the young man rocked in the storm-tossed boat.

Breaking and eating the bread, drinking the wine of the country, she gave Him His flesh and blood; she prepared the Host for the Mass.

This time of Advent is absolutely essential to our contemplation too.

If we have truly given our humanity to be changed into Christ, it is essential to us that we do not disturb this time of growth.

It is a time of darkness, of faith. We shall not see Christ's radiance in our lives yet; it is still hidden in our darkness; nevertheless, we must believe that He is growing in our lives; we must believe it so firmly that we cannot help relating everything, literally everything, to this almost incredible reality.

This attitude it is which makes every moment of every day and night a prayer.

In itself it is a purification, but without the tense resolution and anxiety of self-conscious aim.

How could it be possible that anyone who was conscious that Christ desired to see the world with his eyes would look willingly on anything evil? Or knowing that He wished to work with his hands, do any work that was shoddy, any work that was not as near perfection as human nature can achieve?

Who, knowing that his ears must listen for Christ, could listen to blasphemy or to the dreary dirtiness of so much of our conversation, or could fail to listen to the voice of a world like ours with compassion?

Above all, who, knowing that Christ asked for his heart to love with, for his heart to bear the burden of the love of God, could fail to discover that in every pulsation of his own life there is prayer?

This Advent awareness does not lead to a selfish preoccupation with self; it does not exclude outgoing love to others—far from it. It leads to them inevitably, but it prevents such acts and words of love from becoming distractions. It makes the very doing of them reminders of the Presence of Christ in us.

It is through doing them that we can preserve the secrecy of Advent without failing to offer the loveliness of Christ in us to others.

Everyone knows how terrible it is to come into contact with those people who have an undisciplined missionary urge, who, having received some grace, are continually trying to force the same grace on others, to *compel* them not only to be converted but to be converted in the same way and with precisely the same results as themselves.

Such people seem to wish to dictate to the Holy Ghost. God is to inspire their neighbour to see things just as they do, to join the same societies, to plunge into the same activities. They go about like the scriptural monster, seeking whom they may devour. They insist that their victims have obvious vocations to assist in, or even be completely sacrificed to, their own interests. Very often they unwittingly tear out the tender little shoot of Christ-life that was pushing up against the dark heavy clay, and when the poor victim has been devoured, he is handed over, spiritless and broken, as a predigested morsel for the next one-hundred-per-cent zealot who comes along.

Our Lady's example is very different from this.

When a woman is carrying a child she develops a certain instinct of self-defence. It is not selfishness; it is not egoism. It is an absorption into the life within, a folding of self like a little tent around the child's frailty, a God-like instinct to cherish, and some day to bring forth, the life. A closing upon it like the petals of a flower closing upon the dew that shines in its heart.

This is precisely the attitude we must have to Christ, the Life within us, in the Advent of our contemplation.

We could scrub the floor for a tired friend, or dress a wound for a patient in a hospital, or lay the table and wash up for the family; but we shall not do it in martyr spirit or with that worse spirit of self-congratulation, of feeling that we are making *ourselves* more perfect, more unselfish, more positively kind.

We shall do it just for one thing, that our hands make Christ's hands in our life, that our service may let Christ serve through us, that our patience may bring Christ's patience back to the world.

By His own will Christ was dependent on Mary during Advent: He was absolutely helpless; He could go nowhere but where she chose to take Him; He could not speak; her breathing was His breath; His heart beat in the beating of her heart.

To-day Christ is dependent upon men. In the Host He is literally put into a man's hands. A man must carry Him to the dying, must take Him into the prisons, work-houses, and hospitals, must carry Him in a tiny pyx over the heart on to the field of battle, must give Him to little children and "lay Him by" in His "leaflight" house of gold.

The modern world's feverish struggle for unbridled, often unlicensed, freedom is answered by the bound, enclosed helplessness and dependence of Christ—Christ in the womb, Christ in the Host, Christ in the tomb.

This dependence of Christ lays a great trust upon us. During this tender time of Advent we must carry Him in our hearts to wherever He wants to go, and there are many places to which He may never go unless we take Him to them.

None of us knows when the loveliest hour of our life is striking. It may be when we take Christ for the first time to that grey office in the city where we work, to the wretched lodging of that poor man who is an out-cast, to the nursery of that pampered child, to that battle-ship, airfield, or camp.

Charles de Foucauld, a young French soldier of our own day, became a priest and a hermit in the desert, where he was murdered by some of the Arabs whom he had come to serve. His life as a missionary hermit seemed no more than a quixotic spiritual adventure, a tilting at windmills on the desert sands, but he knew and said that it was worthwhile for just one thing: because he was there the Sacred Host was there.

It mattered nothing if the heroic priest could not utter the wonder that was in his heart; the Blessed Sacrament was there in the desert; Christ was there, silent, helpless, dependent on a creature; that which His servant could not utter in words Christ would utter, in His own time, in silence.

Sometimes it may seem to us that there is no purpose in our lives, that going day after day for years to this office or that school or factory is nothing else but waste and weariness. But it may be that God has sent us there because but for us Christ would not be there. If our being there means that Christ is there, that alone makes it worth while.

There is one exquisite incident in Our Lady's Advent in which this is clearly seen: the Visitation.

"And Mary rising up in those days went into the hill country with haste, into a city of Juda."

How lyrical that is, the opening sentence of St. Luke's description of the Visitation. We can feel the rush of warmth and kindness, the sudden urgency of love that sent that girl hurrying over the hills. "Those days" in which she rose on that impulse were the days in which Christ was being formed in her, the impulse was His impulse.

Many women, if they were expecting a child, would refuse to hurry over the hills on a visit of pure kindness. They would say they had a duty to themselves and to their unborn child which came before anything or anyone else.

The Mother of God considered no such thing. Elizabeth was going to have a child, too, and although Mary's own child was God, she could not forget Elizabeth's need—almost incredible to us, but characteristic of her.

She greeted her cousin Elizabeth, and at the sound of her voice, John quickened in his mother's womb and leapt for joy.

"I am come," said Christ, "that they may have life, and may have it more abundantly." Even before He was born His presence gave life.

With what piercing shoots of joy does this story of Christ unfold ! First the conception of a child in a child's heart, and then this first salutation, an infant leaping for joy in his mother's womb, knowing the hidden Christ and leaping into life.

How did Elizabeth herself know what had happened to Our Lady ? What made her realize that this little cousin who was so familiar to her was the mother of her God ?

She knew it by the child within herself, by the quickening into life which was a leap of joy.

If we practise this contemplation taught and shown to us by Our Lady, we will find that our experience is like hers.

If Christ is growing in us, if we are at peace, recollected, because we know that however insignificant our life seems to be, from it He is forming Himself; if we go with eager wills, "in haste," to wherever our circumstances compel us, because we believe that He desires to be in that place, we shall find that we are driven more and more to act on the impulse of His love.

And the answer we shall get from others to those impulses will be an awakening into life, or the leap into joy of the already wakened life within them.

It is not necessary at this stage of our contemplation to speak to others of the mystery of life growing in us. It is only necessary to give ourselves to that life, all that we are, to pray without ceasing, not by a continual effort to concentrate our minds but by a growing awareness that Christ is being formed in our lives from what we are. We must trust Him for this, because it is not a time to see His face, we must possess Him secretly and in darkness, as the earth possesses the seed. We must not try to force Christ's growth in us, but with a deep gratitude for the light burning secretly in our darkness, we must fold our concentrated love upon Him like earth, surrounding, holding, and nourishing the seed.

We must be swift to obey the winged impulses of His Love, carrying Him to wherever He longs to be; and those who recognize His presence will be stirred, like Elizabeth, with new life. They will know His presence, not by any special beauty or power shown by us, but in the way that the bud knows the presence of the light, by an unfolding in themselves, a putting forth of their own beauty.

It seems that this is Christ's favourite way of being recognized, that He prefers to be known, not by His own human features, but by the quickening of His own life in the heart, which is the response to His coming.

When John recognized Him, He was hidden in His mother's womb. After the Resurrection He was known, not by His familiar features, but by the love in Magdalene's heart, the fire in the hearts of the travellers to Emmaus, and the wound in His own heart handled by Thomas.

At this point there is a question which will occur to a great many people. It is this: does this experience of Advent occur once in a lifetime or many times?

The answer is that this depends upon the dealings of the Holy Spirit with each separate soul but that usually it occurs many times.

The whole cycle of Our Lady's contemplation is a great circle of rhythmic light; some people can complete it year after year by a deliberate living through the liturgical seasons of the Church, renewing their Advent with the Advent of the Church.

To others it comes in different ways. Often, conversion to the Faith, or to a more living awareness of the

Faith, is the occasion of the first Advent of the soul. For what is conversion but the *fiat* of Our Lady echoed again and the conception of Christ in yet another heart ?

Besides these passive and partly passive Advents, there are Advents in the details of our life, details of immense importance of which life is made up.

First of all—work.

The great tragedy that has resulted from modern methods of industry is that the creativeness of Advent has been left out of work.

Production no longer means a man making something that he has conceived in his own heart.

It usually means a great many men making part of something which is no part of themselves and in which, by an ironical paradox, they have no part.

Even when one man makes the whole of one thing, he usually has to compete with a machine and therefore to make it against time—which is only a way of saying to make it against nature.

No man should ever make anything except in the spirit in which a woman bears a child, in the spirit in which Christ was formed in Mary's womb, in the love with which God created the world.

The integral goodness and fittingness of the work of a man's hands or mind is sacred.

He must have it in his heart to make it. His imagination must see it, and its purpose, before it exists in material.

His whole life must be disciplined to gain and keep the skill to make it.

He must, having conceived it, allow it to grow within him, until at last it flows from him and is woven of his life and is the visible proof that he has uttered his *fiat*: "Be it done unto me according to thy word !"

Yes, according to the will of God, as an expression of the love of God.

So that it is possible to whisper in wonder and awe, and without irreverence, on seeing the finished work: "The Word is made flesh."

Every work that we do should be a part of the Christ forming in us which is the meaning of our life, to it we must bring the patience, the self-giving, the time of secrecy, the gradual growth of Advent.

This Advent in work applies to all work, not only that which produces something permanent in time but equally to the making of a carving in wood or stone or of a loaf of bread. It applies equally to the making of a poem and to the sweeping of a floor.

The permanency in it is in the generation of Christ-life. That outlasts time itself. It is eternal.

It is not only in work, in the realization of Faith, and in conscious prayer that we need the season of Advent; we need it in suffering, in joy, and in thought.

We need it in everything that is to bear fruit in our lives.

People sometimes get disheartened because they have read that suffering ennobles and have met people who seem to have come out of the crucible like pure silver, made beautiful by suffering; but it seems to them that in their own case it is quite the opposite. They find that, however hard they try not to be, they are irritable; that astonishing stabs of bitterness afflict them, that far from being more sympathetic, more understanding, there is a numbness, a chill on their emotions: they cannot respond to others at all; they seem not to love anyone any more; and they even shrink from, and dread the very presence of, those who are compassionate and who care for them.

They say that in their case suffering is certainly a failure.

The truth is that they are too impatient to wait for the season of Advent in sorrow to run its course; a seed contains all the life and loveliness of the flower, but it contains it in a little hard black pip of a thing which even the glorious sun will not enliven unless it is buried under the earth.

There must be a period of gestation before *anything* can flower.

If only those who suffer would be patient with their early humiliations and realize that Advent is not only the time of growth but also of darkness and hiding and waiting, they would trust, and trust rightly, that Christ is growing in their sorrow, and in due season all the fret and strain and tension of it will give place to a splendour of peace.

The same with joy; we sometimes accuse young people of grasping joy and not realizing their blessings and not being made bigger and kinder and lovelier as they ought to be by all delight.

Joy also must be allowed to gestate.

Everyone should open his heart very wide to joy, should welcome it and let it be buried very deeply in him; and he should wait the flowering of it with patience. Of course, the first ecstasy will pass, but because in real joy Christ grows in us, the time will come when joy will put forth shoots and the richness and sweetness of the person who rejoiced will be Christ's flowering.

We must never forget that it is the Holy Spirit who sows this Christ-seed in us, and the Spirit of Wisdom, Light, Truth is given to us in countless ways. For example, through books, through the spoken word, through music and pictures, through almost every possible experience; but we often refuse the Holy Spirit the Advent season.

We live in an age of impatience, an age which in everything, from learning the ABC to industry, tries to cut out and do away with the natural season of growth. That is why so much in our life is abortive.

We ought to let everything grow in us, as Christ grew in Mary. And we ought to realize that in everything that does grow quietly in us, Christ grows. We should let thoughts and words and songs grow slowly and unfold in darkness in us.

There are things that refuse to be violated by speed, that demand at least their proper time of growth; you can't, for example, cut out the time you will leave an apple pie in the oven. If you do, you won't have an apple pie.

If you leave a thought, a chance word, a phrase of music, in your mind, growing and cherished for its proper season, you will have the wisdom or peace or strength that was hidden in that seed.

In this contemplation there is great virtue in practising patience in small things until the habit of Advent returns to us.

Sometimes this Advent season of the soul is a recurring rhythm through life, deliberately chosen as such or simply given to us. Sometimes it is the immediate result of conversion or of a new awareness of God or of an increase of Love.

Sometimes it is a painful experience. It may be that a soul brimmed with love becomes dumb, inarticulate, blind, seeing only darkness, unable to give things that it longs to give to a world of children asking for bread.

This simply means that the Holy Spirit of Love, by which Christ was conceived in that heart, is compelling it to suffer the period of growth.

The light is shining in the darkness, but the darkness does not comprehend it.

To a soul in such a condition, peace will come as soon as it turns to Our Lady and imitates her. In her the Word of God chose to be silent for the season measured by God. She, too, was silent; in her the light of the world shone in darkness. To-day, in many souls, Christ asks that He may grow secretly, that He may be the light shining in the darkness.

In the seasons of our Advent—waking, working, eating, sleeping, being—each breath is a breathing of Christ into the world.

PASTORAL

I AM your reed, sweet shepherd, glad to be.
Now, if you will, breathe out your joy in me
And make bright song.
Or fill me with the soft moan of your love
When your delight has failed to call or move
The flock from wrong.

Make children's songs, or any songs to fill
Your reed with breath of life; but at your will
Lay down the flute,
And take repose, while music infinite
Is silence in your heart; and laid on it
Your reed is mute.

PART TWO

" All things were made by him;
and without him was made nothing that was made

In him was life, and the life was the light of men.

And the light shineth in the darkness,
and the darkness did not comprehend it."

(JOHN I, 3–5)

ET HOMO FACTUS EST

HUMANLY speaking, the time of Advent must have been the happiest time in Our Lady's life.

The world about her must have been informed with more than its habitual loveliness, for she was gathering it all to the making of her son.

But sometimes a pang of grief must have shot through her; for example, when the young wheat grew and she saw it pierce the earth with little swords. Perhaps the first sword to pierce her heart was a blade of green wheat.

For was not her precious burden a grain of wheat sown in a field ?

Was He not bread ? The world's bread that must be broken ?

Everything must have spoken to her of Him, as if the beauty of the world was one more prophecy.

To children it seems perfectly natural that God's thoughts should become snow and water and stars; and creation itself is simply His meditation on Christ.

The seed in the earth is the unborn child. The snow on the field is the Virgin Mother's purity. The bloom on the black thorn, flowering through the land, His birth. The falling of the red rose leaves foretells His passion, the wheat is bound in sheaves because He was bound, it is threshed because He was scourged. The fruit is red on the bough because He was crucified; because He rose from the dead, spring returns to us again.

If such is the beauty of the world to ordinary children, what must it have been to the Mother of God, when her whole being was folded upon the unborn Christ within her?

He was completely her own, utterly dependent upon her: she was His food and warmth and rest, His shelter from the world, His shade in the Sun. She was the shrine of the Sacrament, the four walls and the roof of His home.

Yet she must have longed to hold Him between her hands and to look into His human face and to see in it, in the face of God, a family likeness to herself!

Think of that! But perhaps you cannot, unless you happen to be a young priest newly ordained, waiting for the moment when you will hold in your hands the first Host that you have consecrated at your first Mass.

It must have been a season of joy, and she must have longed for His birth, but at the same time she knew that every step that she took, took her little son nearer to the grave.

Each work of her hands prepared His hands a little more for the nails; each breath that she drew counted one more to His last.

In giving life to Him she was giving Him death.

All other children born must inevitably die; death belongs to fallen nature; the mother's gift to the child is life.

But Christ *is* life; death did not belong to Him.

In fact, unless Mary would give Him death, He could not die.

Unless she would give Him the capacity for suffering, He could not suffer.

He could only feel cold and hunger and thirst if she gave Him *her* vulnerability to cold and hunger and thirst.

He could not know the indifference of friends or treachery or the bitterness of being betrayed unless she gave Him a human mind and a human heart.

That is what it meant to Mary to give human nature to God.

He was invulnerable; He asked her for a body to be wounded.

He was joy itself; He asked her to give Him tears.

He was God; He asked her to make Him man.

He asked for hands and feet to be nailed.

He asked for flesh to be scourged.

He asked for blood to be shed.

He asked for a heart to be broken.

The stable at Bethlehem was the first Calvary.

The wooden manger was the first Cross.

The swaddling bands were the first burial bands.

The Passion had begun.

Christ was man.

This, too, was the first separation.

This was her son, but now He was outside of Her: He had a separate heart: He looked at the world with the blind blue eyes of a baby, but they were His own eyes.

The description of His birth in the Gospel does not say that she held Him in her arms but that she "wrapped Him up in swaddling clothes and laid Him in a manger."

As if her first act was to lay Him on the Cross.

She knew that this little son of hers was God's Son and that God had not given Him to her for herself alone but for the whole world.

This is one of the greatest of all the things that we must learn from our contemplation of Our Lady.

Few mothers realize that their children are part of a whole and that the whole is the family of God, to whom every child born owes all the love and service of a brother or sister.

Many mothers try to shield their children from the common life, to give them a sheltered upbringing, so to shield them from all risk of sickness or pain or poverty that they are shielded from vitality and the vast experience of living.

They hate to see them grow or experience anything that will make them independent.

Sometimes a possessive mother even grudges a child his dream kingdom.

I remember a little boy who was punished for daydreaming. His dream kingdom was a deep green forest peopled by wizards and gnomes and magic children but where no grown-up people could come. Here he was king. But when I saw him his white face was dirty with tears, and his mother explained that she had punished him because when she asked for his attention, he was "so far away."

Many women feel the same fear and resentment of the Kingdom of God, particularly as the boy who adventures into that kingdom will have to take up arms, to face ardours and endurances, to make sacrifices; and if ever he is crowned, it will be with thorns.

Two things afflict the mother who resents this. One is that her child should suffer and even, it seems, suffer through his own fault. The other is that he should escape from her; in that kingdom he is alone and independent; like the dreaming little boy, he is (or seems to be) "so far away."

Our Lady knew that her little boy would inhabit a secret kingdom and suffer and die to be crowned in it.

She did not want to take back anything of her gift of herself or take away one tittle of His suffering from Him.

She knew, better than anyone else will ever know it, that the greatest of all griefs is to be unable to mitigate the suffering of one whom we love. But she was willing to suffer that, because that was what He asked of her.

There was no trace of indifference or detachment in Our Lady's attitude. She was not indifferent to Christ's suffering, but there was something that she was deeply aware of which made her more than ready for it.

It was this: that little shivering mite in the manger was her own flesh and blood; her Advent work was done; she had formed Christ of her own life, in herself; and now that she had brought Him forth, she lived in Him.

Quite literally, her life was in Christ.

Therefore there could never be anything He suffered which she did not.

He would suffer and she with Him.

Everyone has the right to the loneliness of his own sorrow.

Christ, who so willingly accepted comfort, sympathy, friendship all through His life, cried out "I thirst" on the Cross.

He meant all thirst. His body was dried up with the terrible thirst that comes from loss of blood and His soul thirsted for the people He was bleeding for, and His heart thirsted for the compassion of His own people.

But when a soldier, moved by compassion, gave Him myrrh to ease His thirst, He tasted it and turned away.

Mary also refused the myrrh.

She would not try to take away His suffering. In this she was more than one with Him; she was one with Him even in His aloneness.

This is another of the things to be discovered in contemplating Our Lady. We ask Him to come and abide in us; we ask the Holy Spirit to form Him from our lives; we believe that He does do this.

If Christ is formed of our lives, it means that He will suffer in us. Or, more truly, we will suffer in Him.

"And He was made man."

Our Lady saw at once what was meant in her case: supernaturally, He was made herself.

If He is made man in you, He will be made *you*; in me, me.

It is extremely difficult to lay hold of this fact. It is very hard not to think of a kind of mystical Christ just beside us, or just in front of us, suffering with infinite patience and joy, being obedient, humble, persevering, fulfilling His Father's will.

It is really difficult to realize that if He is formed in our life we are not beside Him but in Him; and what He asks of us is to realize that it is actually in what *we* do that He wants to act and to suffer.

For example, if you are conscripted, it is Christ Who is saying good-bye and leaving His home; Christ Who is marching on the endless route march. The blisters on the feet of the new recruit are bleeding on the feet of Christ.

Again, if you are an office worker and the person over you is trying, perhaps rather limited in intelligence, so that you imagine you have some kind of right to be irritable, well, it is not you at all that must be obedient and humble and gracious, it is Christ, Christ, Who said to the weak and timid civil servant, Pontius Pilate: "You would have no power over Me if it were not given to you from above."

It really needs to be practised to be understood. We need to say to ourselves a thousand times a day: "Christ wants to do this"; "Christ wants to suffer this."

And we shall thus come to realize that when we resent our circumstances or try to spare ourselves what we should undergo, we are being like Peter when he tried to dissuade Our Lord from the Passion.

There is one tremendous answer to the question which is reiterated to the point of utter weariness: "Why should I?"

It is another question: "Ought not Christ to suffer these things and so enter into His glory?"

THE FUGUE

THE history of the Incarnation is like a fugue, in which the love of God for the world is the ever-recurring motif.

It was uttered first in Mary's voice, in its very simplest phrase, like a few single notes.

A few words spoken to an angel and heard only by him: "Be it done unto me according to thy word."

Then, like the pause that measures music as truly as the sounds, the word of God is silent; for nine months it is inaudible.

It is the pause during which the opening phrase grows within us in loveliness, preparing our minds for the coming splendour.

Suddenly drifting down the darkness, like the bleat of a lamb, comes the cry of a new-born infant.

Now it is no longer Mary's voice uttering the word. Nevertheless it *is* her voice, for it is the human voice that she has given to God.

Now it gathers to delight; it is the sound of laughter in the little house, the sound of a boy's voice at the cottage door, calling to the other children to come out and play.

It grows deeper and is informed with a young man's tenderness, the voice of a shepherd calling his sheep.

Again it is muted and full of tears.

"Jerusalem, Jerusalem, that killest the prophets, and stonest them that are sent to thee, how often would I have gathered thy children as the bird doth her brood under her wings, and thou wouldst not."

It gathers again and is lifted on rising waves of anguish. Christ's "Not my will but thine be done" brings Our Lady's "Be it done unto me according to thy word" to a culminating surrender.

And now it rises and lifts and falls in wave upon wave of sorrow and pity and love, the seven words on the cross ending in the climax of the loud cry before death:

"It is consummated."

"Father, into thy hands I commend my spirit."

Once again the music is measured by silence. Christ is in the tomb as He was in His mother's womb, and just as that first silence was part of the rhythm that moved forward to the visible coming of Life into the world, this silence in the tomb carries the music forward in three great beats to the hour when Life shall again come out of darkness and sweeten and sanctify the world.

Now, as the music becomes audible again, it returns to its simplest form once more. It is lyrical again; at first only a man's breath stirring the flowers in a garden; and then a single word, the name of a friend spoken with indescribable love.

After that it goes on between intervals of silence, in a quiet, serene gentleness, as if it had risen now to the full tide, and all the waves were made one in the flood of a sunlit sea. The words that utter it are all spoken to friends, they are all reassuring, simple and tender. They are all full of a sense of absolute peace.

Many of those who saw Our Lord being taken up into heaven after His Resurrection must have thought that the speaking of God's love on earth was now ended.

Perhaps someone would record what he could remember of His teaching, and for a few generations His words would be told from mouth to mouth, as old fairy stories are told to children.

One person knew that the utterance would go on and that it would still follow the same musical law.

When Our Lady went to visit her cousin in the "hilly country," everything seemed to be vibrant with joy; there was little John the Baptist, who very nearly danced into life; there was Elizabeth, dumbfounded with delight; and Our Lady herself broke out into a song of sheer joy:

" . . . my spirit hath rejoiced in God my Saviour.

"Because he hath regarded the humility of his handmaid; for behold from henceforth all generations shall call me blessed.

"Because he that is mighty hath done great things to me; and holy is his name.

"And his mercy is from generation unto generation. . . ."

This indeed was the Bride of the Spirit speaking.

God had taken His little reed into His hands and the breath of His love sang through it, and this utterance would go on for all generations.

In giving her humanity to God, Mary gave *all* humanity to Him, to be used for His own will.

In wedding her littleness to the Spirit of Love, she wed *all* lowliness to the Spirit of Love.

In surrendering to the Spirit and becoming the Bride of Life, she wed God to the human race and made the whole world pregnant with the life of Christ.

"I am come," Christ said, "that they may have life, and may have it more abundantly."

Mary knew in what the joy of the world was to consist, what it would be that would make everyone call her blessed, for it would simply be her own joy.

Everyone who wished it could be wed to the Spirit: not only solitaries living in lonely cells but everyone in the world; not only young girls and boys or children who had been somehow spared from sin, but sinners too; not only the young but also the old: because the Spirit makes everything new. The life filling her own being, the life leaping in little John the Baptist, the life breaking out into her jubilant song, the life springing on the hills around her—all that would be given to everyone who asked for it.

She had given mankind the key. Indeed, she had unlocked and opened the door of every heart. Now men had only to leave it open.

It seems strange, if we look at it superficially, to say that Our Lady wed the world to the Spirit of Life and that everyone, young and old, can be made new, can be filled with the wonder of Christ-life and bear the green leaf of an ever-returning spring in his spirit.

It seems a strange thing to say. Almost ironical, because our civilization seems to be wedded, not to life, but to death.

At this moment—while I am writing these words—all

the countries in the world are giving all their time and energy to killing.

The young men are either on the battlefields or in the battleships or in bombing planes or else preparing themselves by mock battle.

Millions and millions of pounds are pouring into the making of weapons to kill, not now and then, but every day.

In country after country starvation is setting in or increasing. Children lie down quietly in the streets. Knowing, with a terrible wisdom, that the end has come, they pull their rags round their starved bodies and compose themselves to die.

In the face of all this I sit here in a bombed city and say that because a girl surrendered herself to God two thousand years ago, human nature can be constantly new; life always young; and everyone bring not death into the world but the miraculous life of the Spirit: everyone a bearer of Christ into the world.

If the life that Christ came to give was only natural life, if the peace He promised was the world's peace, of course it would be sheer nonsense to make such a statement.

But we know well that Christ's life and Christ's peace are much stronger, much more enduring and much more real, than the world's life and peace.

We have to remember and to keep on stressing this: that Our Lady is, first of all, the Spirit's Bride; then, as the result of that, the Mother of Life; and that she has made *humanity*, first of all, the Spirit's bride and after that the life-bearer.

Just as no one can have an ordinary child of flesh and blood without there being a union of flesh and blood first, no one can generate spiritual life without first having union with the Spirit.

Marriage, which seems to us to be such a wonderful consummation of love, is only a faint shadow, a kind of symbol, of the wedding of the Spirit of God to humanity;

and it is from that wedding that Christ is born into the world.

Now the union with the Holy Spirit means that the Spirit infuses His qualities into us. He sows us with wonderful seed, His gifts and fruits.

When I hear "Gifts and Fruits" of the Spirit, I always think of the catechism class and the flutter of hands going up when we were asked who knew them—hands flung up like a flight of startled birds—pink English hands and the golden hands of the French pupils.

Some of us managed to get through the lists; most of us stumbled and were prompted; but I am afraid hardly any of us ever understood the words' significance. They were rather difficult, and partly because they were presented to us in the first place simply as lists of words, we soon forgot all about them.

Now, however, because they are our urgent need, we begin to remember them and to realize that Christ is born into the world in lives that have received those qualities.

Were it not so, I think that there would be no hope for us.

When we think about what they are, it becomes very obvious that it was not into the Garden of Eden that Christ would be born, not into a smooth happy world; and that when He was born again, in life after life, it would always be in order to live through the same things as He did the first time: fear, poverty, exile, work, publicity, temptation, pain, betrayal, and crucifixion.

It is obvious, too, that He intended to overcome all this in each person's life, not by doing away with it, but by transforming it; and to overcome death itself by dying.

It is clear, too, that from all eternity the Holy Spirit knew that our Passion in Christ would be in the "dry wood."

Clear, too—from the joy of the Magnificat—that Our Lady knew that her son's reassurance: "Fear not, for I have overcome the world" would echo through all the ages.

For she had opened the door to the Spirit and let the hearts of the coming Christ-bearers receive such gifts as fortitude, peace, patience, long-suffering, humility, and love.

Experience has taught us that war simplifies life. Every individual would experience some equivalent of the Passion even if there were no war; but war makes it visible and even simple, and shows us how the Passion of Christ can be each one's individual secret and at the same time something shared by the whole world.

It is a moment in which the world needs great draughts of supernatural life, needs the Christ-life to be poured into it, as truly and as urgently as a wounded soldier drained of his blood needs a blood transfusion.

In many souls, for this very reason, Christ will say: "It was for *this* hour that I came into this world."

Because only individuals can bear Christ.

Only Christ-bearers can restore the world to life and give humanity back the vitality of love.

No league or conference or committee or group can put life into the world: it can only be born into the world, and only individuals can give birth.

We can give birth to Christ only by unity with the Holy Spirit.

It was because she was aware of how many unknown people would be wed to the Spirit, that Our Lady sang joyfully on the hills while her little unborn cousin leaped for joy.

"His mercy is from generation to generation." At every baptismal font the Infant Christ cries. Every mother soothes Him when her baby cries in hunger, cold, or pain.

In the laughter of all children, the Boy Christ laughs. Every young man speaks with the Shepherd's voice.

It is heard in the hesitating sermons of young priests;

in the whispers of absolution; in the pleadings of human love.

Over all the cities of the world Christ is weeping: "Had you but known the things that are to your peace."

His tears are falling over London, New York, Paris, Berlin, Warsaw, Stalingrad, Moscow, Tokio, Helsinki, Bucharest, Athens, Rome.

Over all the cities of the world.

The voice from the Cross speaks in the desert, in the hospital, from the open seas, from every place where young men are giving their lives.

Mary hears the voice of her son in all these voices, and they echo her *fiat*.

She rejoices because she knows that His will, to which they have surrendered, is that they should have life; that life will prevail in them, in each one of them; and that death is powerless against the risen Christ.

She hears the sweetness of the familiar voice of her child in each one, from cradle to grave. Sometimes she hears it as the great chorus. The motif, first uttered by her in a single sentence, spreads, expands, opens out like a wing. The music gathers from age to age: sometimes it is hammered and beaten out; sometimes it is in time to marching armies; sometimes it is a full orchestra; sometimes it is rung out on peals of bells; sometimes it sinks to a murmur and becomes silent. But in the silence not a beat of the love it utters is lost; it is the silence of a soundless sea rising to flood tide; it is a timed silence, the pause in the music that bears the heart along with it as surely as the sound, preparing it for the sudden ease and sweetness of melody. For it always returns to its lyrical simplicity: is always gathered back to its first phrase.

For the fugue is the music of the Word of God, God's spoken Word, telling His love; and the motif is always gathered back to be concentrated again in its first simplicity.

We always come back to the beginning.

In the beginning the love song of God is a folk song.

Folk song is the telling of the whole world's story through the singing of one's man heart.

The Word of God uttered in Christ's human life is a folk song.

In it is all the primal love and joy and sorrow of all the world.

It explains and simplifies all human lives in all times.

We hear it as children playing by the seashore hear the music of the ocean in a little shell.

We hear it in the voices we know best: our own children's voices, the voices of our parents, wives, husbands, and friends.

We hear it in laughter and tears, tuned to the dullness of our hearing, tuned to the beating of our hearts.

We hear it as sweet and clear as bird's song in Nazareth.

The song of the Incarnation is a folk song.

It is the song of the mother rocking the cradle.

It is the song of the children singing their nursery rhymes.

It is the song of the shepherd calling his sheep.

It is the song of the lover standing at the door.

It is the song of the bridegroom singing to the bride.

WOODEN BAMBINO

THIS is the Christ;
This is the beautiful King,
Swaddled and stiff,
Like a little stark, dead thing.

Carved out of wood,
Still half submerged in the tree;
This is the pain
Of Life, that is Death-for-me.

Secret the smile
On the mouth of the Undefiled,
Terrible, sweet,
Like the smile of a just-dead child.

Secret the smile,
Curved in the eyes while they sleep,
Still, wooden Peace
Of a Babe too old to weep.

Stiff on the breast,
Folded and helpless the hands,
And side by side
Feet in the swaddling bands.

Infinite Love,
Helpless and dumb and still;
Secret, it is
Of His imperious will.

This is the Christ;
This is the beautiful King,
Swaddled and stiff,
Like a little stark, dead thing.

ET VERBUM CARO FACTUM EST

IT seems to me very difficult for people to realize that
the Word is made flesh.

First of all, the flesh is a stumbling block. There are
two schools of thought: one thinks (or feels) that the
flesh is wholly bad; the other, that it is absolutely good.

Even those who accept the revelation on this matter
do not always accept it altogether: their intellects accept
it, but emotionally they do not accept it at all.

Many people do not use their intellect—excepting once or twice in their lifetime—to accept truths which they know that they must. They put these truths away in some sort of drawer in the mind and leave them there. They feel that they have done their duty and that the truth in question is quite useless save to be accepted and put away.

It is rather like having to accept an old hat from our grandmother, who will leave us a fortune so long as we respect her old hat. The idea of wearing the hat is out of the question.

Many people regard the Church as just such a grandmother. She has a fortune, indeed, and we dare not miss it; but she certainly has a lot of funny old hats and shawls and beliefs and traditions, none of which seem to be fashionable or useful or even wearable. However, we accept them in order not to offend the old lady.

Others accept the doctrine that the Word is made flesh with a far more lovely understanding, but they happen to hate flesh and to think it very shocking. And therefore they revolt.

These people are always trying to get away from the flesh altogether and to lead what they call a "spiritual life." But nowadays they are bound to belong to the great army of part-timers; for, with everyone else who is sound, they have to go to work for eight hours every day. And—do what you will with it when you leave the office —you simply have to have your flesh with you while you are there. So the "spiritual life" must be a part-time one !

Sometimes these people carry their fear of the flesh (for hate like this always come from fear) to the extent of hating everything that is beautiful: they resent the fact that beautiful things are used in the service of God: such things as flowers and lights, incense, chrism, linen, wheat and wine.

There are others who allow their fear and repudiation of the flesh to become a vice. They go round the park looking for naked little boys bathing in the Serpentine, in order to hit them with an umbrella or to hand them over to the police.

Others think, or rather, feel (for these reactions are not thought-out but emotional) that the flesh is completely good and requires no heavenly visitation, no indwelling Spirit; for it is, they feel, in itself a kind of God. At least, such is the case with young and reasonably pretty and healthy flesh.

This last attitude is one with which it is easy to be sympathetic, because in the state of primal innocence in which mankind was created, every natural instinct of the flesh tended Godwards. The love of man and woman was a fling of the heart to God. Possibly very much that we call the "aesthetic sense" is, although it misleads us now, a kind of deeply buried inherited memory of innocence, like an old man's memory of his nursery.

The attitude I have just mentioned was more common a generation ago than it is now. There is a tendency now to regard the flesh with contempt, to consider man an animal only and to think very lightly indeed of violating the body.

I have heard sensual indulgence described as "an irresistible bore" by a girl of twenty-two.

There has surely never been an age in which so many people were so particularly preoccupied with their bodies as this age, and yet to so little profit.

To return to the part-time spiritual life: the life of the person who tries to become a saint by being spiritual on her day off. She (and it generally is she) very often wants to get rid of her body or at least of the consciousness of it. She is hard on it, but the hardness is rather of the firm but gentle type than of the fierce. It is negative. She would not treat it, for example, as St. Francis of Assisi did his: he called it an ass, but when the "ass" burned, he went out and rolled in the snow; and when he had received the wounds of Christ upon it and when his eyes had been burnt out with hot irons, he went up a little mountain and sang a glorious song of praise to all the beauty that the poor happy "ass" had brought to him through his senses: "The Song of the Sun."

The part-timer is not aiming at that sort of thing; she aims rather at unfeelingness. In the office she can't help feeling a little. The chairs are so hard and the draughts so continual. But the feeling is not of the worst type, from her point of view, as it is at least unpleasant. She does not like it, but she is not made to feel guilty by it. She is a little over-anxious to consume the proper vitamins, but preferably without relish. Cold mutton and canned pears would be an ideal meal—a meal both nourishing and sense-subduing.

When she has left her body-consciousness in the office and mortified what remains of her senses at supper, she feels that the time has come for prayer, and weary though she is, she tries heroically to pray with what remains of an impotent humanity.

This sounds funny, but actually it is more pathetic than funny. There is so much good in the person, such a desire to adhere to God and such a total misunderstanding both of Him and herself.

The first reason why there is a flaw in all the several attitudes to "the flesh" which I have mentioned, is that so many people think of soul and body as two separate things necessarily in conflict.

Those who idolize the body want, therefore, to be rid of, or at least to deny or forget the existence of, the soul.

Those who despise the body want to subdue it to a condition of unfeelingness, an impotence of sense and emotion and intellect.

Of course, it is true that in human nature there is always a conflict. It is not so much between body and soul as between good and evil, but the body is very often inclined to take the side of evil. It always tends to take the line of least resistance, and that usually results in evil.

Our Lord Himself summed the case up: "The spirit is willing but the flesh is weak."

That the Word was made flesh does mean, however, that the word became human, and a human being *is* a unity of soul and body. It is this substance—humanness, soul and body—in which the Spirit abides and which He wants to change from the weak thing it is to the glorious thing which He intended it to be from the beginning of creation.

Human nature—body and soul. That means so much more than the word "flesh" conveys at first hearing. It means flesh and blood, nerves, the five senses, the sensitive soul, thought, feeling, reactions to other people and to environment—intellect, art, poetry, genius.

Although human beings smear everything they touch, they leave touches of beauty wherever they go, too; evidence that the senses receive their unique gifts of grace, wonder, joy, and gratitude because of the beauty that is their environment.

St. Thomas says that the Being of God is the cause of the beauty of all that is.

The Being of God, then, presses upon man. It is his environment. It sings to him in the winds. When he touches grass or water, he touches it with his fingers; he smells it in fields of hay and clover and in newly cut wood; he listens to it in the falling of the rain and the murmur of the sea. He tastes it in the food that he eats; he sees it in the flowers beneath his feet; he is clothed in it in silk and wool. Its measured beat in his own blood rocks him to sleep with the coming of darkness and wakens him with the light. He receives it in the sunlight like a sacrament that gives life.

If it is thus that the Being of God, given to him through his natural environment, presses so sweetly for entrance to man's spirit through his senses, what limit can there be to the consequences of the Spirit of Life when it has taken possession of him and its light has become the light of his mind and the sight of his eyes?

Even in ignorance, man tends to fall in love with God. He responds to life as he sees it round him with gratitude that becomes love and love that takes shape. For being made in God's image and likeness, man too must look upon the secret of his heart, made visible by the work of his hands.

Therefore he has left this trace of beauty through the ages, from the splendid animals drawn in red earth on the rocks to the intricate cadences of modern poetry.

Primitive man can know and respond to God in his ignorance. If it is thus that man falls in love with the God whom he does not know and responds to Him, what will be the immeasurably greater result of God's falling in love with man, whom He conceived and created for Himself?

In Our Lady God fell in love with humanity.

The Evangelist saw her standing in heaven, clothed in the sun and with her feet upon the moon. Facing the sun, she received its light and gave it back as the moon does.

Something like that has happened to humanity since God made it His bride, through Mary of Nazareth.

"Hallowed be thy name" is a prayer taught to us by Christ. It means "be holy in me," shine out of my heart as the light of the sun shines reflected from the moon, as the bridegroom's glory shines on the face of the bride.

Our Lady gave humanity to God as she gave the water to Christ at Cana, to be changed into wine.

Human nature was to have the qualities of wine: it was to be coloured all through with the splendour of the red blood of Christ; and it was to inebriate, to enliven, to exalt; so that people would infuse life and the sweetness of life into one another.

The most simple manifestation of the Spirit's wedding to the human race is marriage.

Man is restored to his likeness to God when he restores the primal love in him to its morning splendour through Christ—Christ in the man, Christ in the woman. Every moment of their lives is a life-giving to one another.

That the Word was made flesh becomes almost visible in the thought, the work, the restraint, the tenderness, and the embrace through which they give life to one another.

This is no part-time spiritual life, but the prayer without ceasing that we are bidden to.

In the marriage service the bridegroom says to the bride: "With my body I thee worship." It is a perfect act of faith in the indwelling presence of the Spirit.

A man can only worship God; what he can worship in his wife is the Holy Spirit present there, and the Holy Spirit is surely manifest to him in the chastity of her body, in the sweetness of her laughter, in everything which makes her lovable to him.

Neither could he worship her with his body, unless Christ were present in him, for Christ alone can truly worship. The bridegroom comes to the marriage as the priest to the altar, with all the perfection of manhood which the Church asks of Her priests, and the Holy Spirit is manifest in his tenderness to the bride, which restrains and concentrates the tremendous impulse of creative energy, quickened by natural love, just as the law which restricts it gives coherence and beauty to poetry or to music.

What supreme worship marriage is! With it comes a great increase of sanctifying grace, so that all the natural ecstasy and delight of the response of the senses and of the sensitive mind and heart are transformed into the very joy of Christ: and what worship can equal that of gratitude and joy?

The worship of the bridegroom's body is not simply a spark flashed off from the fire of passion that burns out in the wedding season; on the contrary, it pervades his whole life. When he is at work, earning her food and clothes and their home, his concentration of mind, his self-control among his fellow workers, the labour of his hands, his journeying to and from his place of work, his food and sleep and recreation are all expressions of this worship of the bride. All his words of love are words of consecration.

On the night before He died Christ took bread into His hands, blessed and broke it, and gave it to His disciples, saying: "This is my Body."

The Blessed Sacrament is Christ, the whole Christ. He was giving us *Himself*.

In so many other things He laid the stress on the invisible, the immaterial; His kingdom, He said, is not of this earth: His peace is not of this world.

Yet, in giving Himself to the world, He deliberately chose to emphasize the body.

Why?

The body is, for us, the means by which we can give ourselves wholly.

We say: "Go, my thoughts are with you," or "My soul goes with you." And we know that, though something of ourself is with the traveller, essentially we remain separate from him.

We can give someone devoted care, unfailing kindness, and all our worldly possessions, but still we have kept ourselves.

But when we give our body willingly to another as the means of deliberate self-donation, then our union with the other is complete.

We surrender our intimacy, the secret of ourselves, with the giving of our body; and we cannot give it *without* our will, our thoughts, our minds, and our souls.

Christ surrendered the secret of Himself to each one of us when He gave us His Body. In Holy Communion this surrender of the secret of Himself goes on.

"With desire," He said, "have I desired this hour."

The hour when He was to consecrate bread, in order that not only to the whole race would He give His Spirit, but to each individual, the gift of Himself.

He had *longed* for it—that is what the phrase means; longed for the moment when He would give us the Body that Mary had given to Him and for the moment when each one receives Him in Communion. He waited thirty-three years in time for the Last Supper; two thousand years for me.

That taking of bread into His hands, giving Himself through this extremely simple thing, changing this the most natural substance in the world into Himself, and then literally giving Himself with His own hands, was typical of His way with men.

Not only now did He give His body: all His life He had given His body as the expression of His Father's love, the Love which He who is the *Word* had come to express and which could be expressed only by union between God and man in Christ.

These hands that now held out the Host were first given when they fumbled for His Mother's breast in the blue-eyed blindness of babyhood; they were given when He hollowed the palms for the nails, day after day, with the round handle of the wood-worker's mallet; when He laid them upon the sick to heal; when He took the hand of the little daughter of Jairus to lift her up from being dead; when He lifted them up in blessing: the beautiful, hard hands, with their line and sinew of toil.

He gave Himself through His body from the beginning to the end in tears, in sweat, in weariness; with spoken words, with glances of love; walking the dusty roads, visiting the homes of His friends and His enemies; in the gift of His blood.

The part that the pain and privations of His body played in our redemption we know and meditate often: the poverty, the toil, the fasting, the crucifixion.

We think less often of the *joy* that should be ours through Christ's body.

It was the *Word* that was made flesh. Not only did He take our sorrows to Himself, but He gave the delight, the happiness that *He is*, to our humanness.

No man ever enjoyed life as He did. He gathered up the colour, sound, touch, meaning of everything about

Him and united it all to the most exquisite sensitiveness, the most pure capacity for delight.

Most people know the sheer wonder that goes with falling in love, how not only does everything in heaven and earth become new, but the lover himself becomes new. It is literally like the sap rising in the tree, putting forth new green shoots of life. The capacity for joy is doubled, the awareness of beauty sharpened, the power to do and enjoy creative work increased immeasurably. The heart is enlarged, there is more sympathy, more warmth, in it than ever before. The lover's mind is vibrant with his new life, every sense quickened; and while his blood races, an immense power of tenderness makes him so much the ruler and master of all this passion of joy, that he is able to bestow it on another with such restraint, such gentleness, that however frail she is, she can receive it.

This being in love increases a man's life, makes him potent with new life, a life-giver; from it comes all the poetry, music, and art in the world. Man, made in the image of God, must also make the image of his own love. He makes songs and tunes and drawings and poems; children's stories, fairy stories, jewels, dances, and all else that tells the story of his heart long after his heart is dust.

He himself, and his work, is one more manifestation that "the Word was made flesh, and dwelt among us: and we beheld His glory."

Christ on earth was a Man in love.

His love gave life to all loves. He was Love itself. He infused life with all the grace of its outward and inward joyfulness, with all its poetry and song, with all gaiety and laughter and grace.

With His body He united Himself to the world.

We incline to think that the comparison of Christ's oneness with His Church to human marriage is an attempt to find a symbol for *Christ's* love, that the marriage is the greater reality. But it is the other way about: the marriage of man and woman is the dim showing of

the reflected glory of Christ's union through the giving
of Himself, in the flesh, to humanity.

Christ always chose the purest and simplest material
things as the means of giving His grace, which means
giving Himself. Think of the things He used to make
our life sacramental: water, oil, salt, wheat, wine, and
words.

Primitive man left his response to the world about
him on the wall of the cave, drawn in red earth.

Christ has left something like that in the outward
forms of worship and the customs and traditions of the
Church: His response to the world about Him was to
give life through the loveliest and least.

Even the list of contents in the Missal is poetry, poetry
interwoven with the warmth and homeliness of the
Incarnation.

The Church blesses ordinary material things, and each
one of them speaks eloquently of the Divine Lord who
commands Her to bless them.

"Various Blessings," reads the Contents of the Missal:
the Blessing of the Lamb at Easter; of eggs; of bread; of
the fruits of the earth; of any kind of food; of candles.

We can feel the smile of Christ in these blessings,
warming them through and through like the sun shining
in an orchard and saturating the thin leaves with gold.

Each one is a reminder of Him and of something
lyrical or happy in the Incarnation. They take us back to
His childhood:

The little Lamb of God blessing the lambs jumping
in the fields;

The mothering hen sitting on her eggs, seen by the
Boy Christ and remembered when He compared Himself
to a mothering bird;

The bread and the food and the fruits of the earth:
He is the living bread and the food of the Soul.

The candles: He is the light of the world, the light like
sunlight that nourishes, heals, and makes beautiful. Yes,
but He also wishes to be thought of as a candle burning

in a little room—to be the secret light fended in His true home, the narrow human heart.

Even when all His capacity for pain was fulfilled and consummated, Christ did not give up His body: it still exists. It was seen and touched on earth after He rose from the dead; His voice was heard; His foot could still leave its print in the dew on the grass beside His tomb.

On Holy Saturday a burning candle is carried into the church. There is the cry of a man's voice: "*Lumen Christi*"—"The Light of Christ."

There is the blessing of the water, and the breathing upon the water; there is the blessing of oil and chrism for anointing; from the paschal candle, studded with aromatic nails, the altar fires are lit.

Once again bread and wine and water are brought into the sanctuary, and a Host is consecrated.

At the Elevation a peal of little bells rings out.

It is not only worship of the soul, but the soul expressed through the body. The priest prostrates himself, beats his breast, lifts his arms up to heaven, makes the sign of the cross, speaks the mysterious words: "This is my Body."

The congregation joins in this worship, and it is expressed by the body of each one: they know that when the words of consecration are spoken the Word made flesh is there for each one of them; the same glory pours into the difficult worship of the old rheumatic woman at the back of the church as into the priest who is lifting up God in his hands.

The glory of the Incarnation is equally in the aching of the old woman's bones and the young priest's ecstasy.

The glory is not confined to the church where the Mass is offered: it extends in ring upon ring of light and circles the world.

The gift of Christ's Body makes everyone a priest; because everyone can offer the Body of Christ on the altar of his own life.

But the offering must be the offering of a human being who is intensely alive, a potent humanness, great sorrow and great joy, a life lit up with the flame of Love, fierce fasts and thirsts and feasts of sheer joy.

Everyone offering himself to God must offer the glory of life in himself, whether it be through giving it up or rejoicing in it; through a renunciation or an embrace.

Every gesture in life can be one with the gesture of the priest in the Mass.

It is not in making our flesh unfeeling that we hallow God's name on earth but in offering it to God burning with the flame of life. Everything can be put into the fire that Christ came to kindle; and whether it be the bitter wood of sorrow or the substance of joy, it will burn upwards with the same splendour of light.

It is the *Word* that is made flesh, the spirit of joy and wisdom and love. So where the spirit is at home in a human creature, and Christ born of his life is manifest, there must be a grace of living which touches every detail of life. His mind must be quickened; he must see the world in wonder and reverence; he must be conscious that privations, pain, and weariness of the body are prayer; but that so, too, are the pleasures and labours of the body.

Body and soul together give glory to God: the sharper the capacity for sorrow and joy, the greater the hallowing; the subtler the delicacy of the daily life, the surer is Christ proved in it. In office or home or hospital; prison, barracks, or church—anywhere at all where men and women are—the mystery of the Incarnation can bear fruit in bodies and souls all day and all night, too.

The little crippled child who is patient, lying still; the urchin who dances in the gutter to the barrel organ; the soldier in battle; the clerk in the office; the woman dusting her home: in all of them the Word is made flesh; and if we will, we can behold in them His glory, Who is dwelling among us.

A boy of four ran from flower to flower in the garden,

kissing each one, and each time he said: "That's a kiss for God."

Christ laid hold of the world with His human hands; He took it to His human heart; with His body He wed Himself to it. Our life is the response of the bride.

"Lift up your hearts."

"We have lifted them up unto God."

We have thought about the simplicity of the things Christ chose to use, but simplest of all and the first essential was the humanity of Mary of Nazareth, in whose flesh the Word was made flesh.

The marriage feast of the parable is here and now; and everyone has a wedding garment if he will only accept it and put it on.

Christ has laid His Humanity upon us. A seamless garment, woven by a woman, single and complete, coloured like the lilies of the field, passing the glory of Solomon, but simple as the wild flowers. A wedding garment worn to the shape of His body, warm with His life.

PART THREE

"Whither is thy Beloved gone,
O Thou fairest among women?
Whither is thy Beloved turned aside?
That we may seek him with thee."

(*Song of Songs*, vi. 1).

THE LOST CHILD

SURELY there can be no one with a spark of imagination who has not, at some time or other, felt baffled and even hurt by the Gospel record of the loss of the Child Jesus.

The striking thing about it is that it was not really loss. Our Lady did not lose Christ; He deliberately went away. He allowed her to imagine Him safe in the company of travellers; and without a word He slipped away and went back to Jerusalem.

Nor was this an isolated incident. When she had found Him, after three days of utter bereavement, He returned with her to Nazareth; but after what must have seemed a very short time to her, He left her again, and from that time forward her life was a continual seeking for Him.

We hear of her standing outside in the crowd during His public life; of her following Him to the Cross, where the very life she had given Him was taken away from her. For a brief moment He was put into her arms again, and then taken up quickly (for there was urgency over the burial), and put into the tomb.

Why did Christ treat Our Lady in this way?

It was not only to show His absolute trust in her or her trust in Him (although she was the one human being in whom God's Will was completely unhindered). It was because Our Lady lived the life of all humanity. Concentrated into her tiny history is the life story of the

68

whole human race, the whole relationship of the redeemed human race with God.

She led the Christ life perfectly; her life was literally, as ours should be, "in Christ."

Naturally, then, she experienced this loss of the Child, because it is an experience which *we all* have to go through, that our love may be sifted and purified.

This seems unjust, that purity should be purified, but it is the far bigger justice, the logic, of supreme love.

Christ, who was innocence, suffered the sense of guilt, of despair; He exempted Himself from no suffering that sin had inflicted upon human nature; He led the life of every man.

Mary, being one with Him, would not be exempt from any human experience: she did not live the perfect Christ-life in privileged circumstances or ask for exemptions from the common lot.

The Purification in the temple (which scandalizes many people) proves her willingness to purify purity. She went among all the other women and made the offering of the poor: two doves.

But during her whole life she accepted everything which in our case is a necessary purification but in her case was the proof that she loved us with Christ's love.

She knew the anxieties of all poor women wondering how to clothe and feed their children. Her son's Godhead may well have made Him as puzzling and disturbing to the natural mother in her as all other adolescents are to their mothers.

But since they were one, and since only His love for us measured hers, all this had to be; in it is the secret of her heroism; of her strength in being able to see Him suffer. It was because His suffering was hers. And therefore, even being parted, even death, which gave her the sense of loss, could not really part them, could not *separate* them, any more than the breaking of a Host in two can separate or divide Christ.

She lived in Him; her life was in His; her flesh and blood was in His; her will was in His. Unless He took her flesh and blood out of His hands and feet, He had to let her hands and feet be nailed in His.

Christ suffered the sense of the loss of God, of being left, *forsaken* by God.

Our Lady, therefore, suffered the same thing: the sense of the loss of God. And of all the sufferings of human nature, this is the most universal and the most purifying.

Therefore she lived through this strange, baffling thing for the love of God and for the love of us; she suffered it in Christ because Christ suffers it in human nature.

We have seen that her "Be it done unto me according to thy word" is uttered again in His "Not my will, but thine be done." Just so is her "Son, why hast thou done so to us?" repeated in His "My God, My God, why hast thou forsaken me?"

Everyone experiences this sense of the loss of the Divine Child.

Everyone knows it in different ways and in different degrees.

Converts, and others who have received some great revivifying grace, find the springtime of their souls suddenly chill. The uprush and thrust of spring fails, and they are left empty.

It does indeed seem to them that the Child was born into their lives; filled the little house of their souls with His laughter: and now, without warning, He is gone.

There is no emptiness like the emptiness of the house from which a child has gone away.

There are others who perhaps have never known the vivid joy of conversion or the conscious reception of special graces; who have not had any extraordinary sweetness or realization of God in their lives; but almost imperceptibly it has become harder for them to pray; their minds revert less and less often to God; they begin to realize that religion bores them; and then, one day, they find in themselves a terrible grey, bleak loneliness for which they cannot account.

A Catholic who had never been inside any but a Catholic church was taken to see a pre-Reformation cathedral now in Anglican hands. It was filled with fine old carving, the tombs of Crusaders, a famous pulpit and font, and so on, but she was struck only by one thing: the emptiness: the absence of the Blessed Sacrament.

"But it is empty!" was all she could say.

Until that time she had not had any special devotion to the Blessed Sacrament, but from that day her devotion began.

In the same way some people remain unaware of the real presence in the soul until they become sharply aware of the sense of real absence.

Another way in which we experience the loss, or the sense of loss, of the Child is in our moods.

People of every sort have rhythmic cycles of moods, passing from happiness to sadness, from faith to gloom, from cheer to depression.

One day they are brilliantly gay; the world shines; they want to sing. The next day (or the next week) something has gone out of the music; the world is flat.

Such moods occur rhythmically and are independent of circumstance. They are among the many natural means that God uses in His dealings with men.

So, in their natural moods—and even when they do not know it—the typists and clerks and shop assistants and clergymen and cabinet ministers (and all the rest who have what they probably call' "the blues"), or the soldiers, sailors, and airmen who are "browned off," are sharing in the experience of Our Lady's sense of loss when the Child Christ left her and went without her back to Jerusalem.

Another way in which we lose Him is through sin. Some feel this keenly; the loss tears them. Others are hardly aware of it. But His absence gradually changes them, and every trace of His likeness disappears. They can be compared to old photographs. You know what a pitiful thing the photograph of a long dead person is: it yellows with age and grows dingy; it "dates," it loses that person's living personality and retains only some reminder of something of his or her time which now seems ridiculous, such as an old-fashioned hat or dress. The photograph itself seems dead. In fact, the longer we stare, the more impossible we find it to recall the living face.

I once saw an old, old woman shaking the photograph of her long dead husband, while tears, which seemed literally to hiss from her eyes, blistered it. "It won't smile at me; it won't speak to me"; she said: "and I have *forgotten* his face."

Some feel the loss most keenly in their own souls, others experience it through other people.

There is the most obvious thing; death. Someone who seemed to take the place of God in our life—a mother or brother, an adored husband, an irreplaceable friend; in them we saw all that proved God's love to us, and they have died.

Or we may have idealized someone and seen in him, as we thought, the very quintessence of the Christ-life. Something happens which shatters our conception; and suddenly it seems to us that Christ is extinguished in him.

It is not only in people. The sense of the joy in anything is the sense of Christ's presence. (For in evil no one ever yet knew the true sense of joy.)

Our work may be for us a daily manifestation of the Word made flesh—such as the work of a carver. And if it is cut out of our lives by circumstance, once again the sense of transforming life is snatched away.

Sometimes He is lost in the loss of a vocation.

When we were young, or when Faith was young in us, we were aware of the call within us, of the Holy Spirit inspiring us to lead the austere life of sacrifice and uncompromising charity which is the only really free and fetterless life on earth. Then, indeed, there was space, light, and air in us. But we have gradually frittered away the vocation to be free. Long ago we really were contented with one coat. We did not worry about money, even though we had none; in fact, more *because* we had none. Poverty was lyrical, and it safeguarded humility. The man who is truly and merrily poor and little, glad to be so, is charitable. He loves because he is loved. It is almost as much the duty of a Christian to be loved as to love: the happily poor man achieves both.

We were once that poor man. But gradually we have frittered our freedom away: always increasing our wants, little by little making more and more necessities for ourselves; forming habit after habit of petty indulgence; until one day (if we are given the grace of realizing it), we discover that we too have lost the Divine Child. The lyrical young Christ that was the youth of our soul has gone away, leaving us a dyspeptic old man, lonely in a cluttered room of his own making, a forgotten invalid sitting in a timeless twilight of mediocrity.

But it happens as often in following as in losing a vocation. Perhaps we were called to found, to organize, or to lead some little movement or society or a group in an existing society, or to take charge of a hospital or club or post—any such thing. We started with the one idea of serving God, but gradually the formalities, the necessary social life, the business side, has overcome us. From being an apostle we have become an organizer; from being an organizer, a business man or woman.

The world of the society or group becomes our whole world; our little job assumes a ridiculous importance; we lose sight of the Universe; and presently that little world of ours—did we but know it—resembles a beehive where the queen is continually stroked and flattered and soothed by the others to keep her going. Once again we have been untrue to the first love and have lost the Divine Child.

For some people, the sense of loss is almost permanent:

it may go on for years; it may end only in death. Yet, also, it may end at any moment.

In some it is for short intervals, alternated with the unforeseen sweetness of His return. He goes without warning, and they know no reason; but the house is empty. Then, as suddenly, He is "there in the midst."

But whether it be for a long or a short time, a searing grief or one that wears the mind and heart gradually, the experience itself is universal; and if one thing stands out particularly in the case of very devout people, it is that in them you can see that it is not a loss but His deliberate going away. They pray, they meditate, they deny themselves; they perform all the works of mercy; nevertheless, Christ seems to leave them.

In some cases the loss is profound, it is a complete aridity; not only the sense of the empty house, but loss like loss of sun and rain from the roots of a tree, a drying up, a withering of heart and mind; a root starvation for life; something for which there are no words but which ages of men have called, for a name's sake, "dryness," or "aridity of the soul."

With others, the fact that the loss is almost light is in itself an aggravation to the loneliness. The child's absence fills the heart with his recent presence, like the echo of his voice still ringing through the empty room, or his little robe on the chair, still warm from the touch of his body. He seems to be just out of reach. It is impossible to accept his absence; yet the only movement in the house is the door closing behind him.

Things which happen to individuals happen to nations as nations. In these days we see how nations have personality and become people to us; it is the martyr-nations of the world that have revealed this. We cannot think of Poland as a country any more, but only as a person. That is because only a person can have tears on her cheeks and wear the crown of thorns. Greece and Czechoslovakia are martyr-countries: they are people because of their martyrdom, and because compassion has made us love them. A sailor calls his ship "she," never "it," for he loves his ship: therefore, it becomes a person to him.

England, as a nation, is also going through the experience of the loss of the Divine Child.

The Christ Child in a nation is like the presence of the child in the house: everything centres upon his youth; and he fills everything with his life. If he goes away, the child's values go, too, such as the sense of wonder, mystery, beauty, and adventure: the poetry which, free from materialism, is the most complete realism.

In England there are traces of where the Child once lived: there are remnants of the Faith; but not the certainty of the Faith that there once was. There is a wistful longing to believe; but not the joyful freedom of living in belief. There is the desire to set up laws of justice for everyone's happiness; but not the spirit of the Child's obedience to God's Law in the heart of all men: and indeed without that no codes and laws can have value; because those who make them have not the capacity to keep them.

The absence of supernatural joy on our feast days shows more than anything else that the Divine Child is absent. Christmas is no longer Christ's birthday, except to a few people. It is no longer the time in which everyone, young and old, is born again; no longer the time when the instinct is to find a *home* where there is a Christmas tree, lit up with tinsel and little candles and with a crowned bambino on top of it; and children standing at the foot of the tree, looking at it with faces suffused with joy.

That is gone, except in a few homes. To most people, Christmas is a time in which to eat an enormous meal and get drunk, and that is all.

Good Friday is a holiday, and nothing else, for the majority: it is the day on which there is more drunkenness than on any other day in the year. An English fair is one of the most glorious things in the world, even on Hampstead Heath, with its jingling round-abouts, striped booths, coconut shies, gypsy fortune-tellers, and its riot of friendliness. But the fair on Hampstead Heath on Good Friday makes Hampstead Heath Calvary, a Calvary where Christ is mocked while He dies. But His own excuse for poor human nature is true indeed: "they *know* not."

Something remains of the Child's presence: we cherish a kind of gentleness, a tolerance which is uniquely English and which springs in its origin from Christianity.

All that is good in our national life started in Christianity, and our dogged holding fast to tradition is partly because our traditions, even when they have now worn a little absurd, were originally customs of logical Christian living.

We still feel our Mother's hand in the darkness and tighten our grip of it.

Our old cathedrals and our little Saxon churches are empty: nevertheless, they are like the nests of birds that have migrated, and they have not quite lost the warmth of the fledgling's breast and the mother's wings.

When spring returns, and the birds come back, they come to the same tree, the same branch, the same nest, that they left: we still pray with hope that our Dove will come back to us.

England was once the nest of the Pelican, once Our Lady's dowry. Where the Mother of God walked in English fields, the print of her little Son's footsteps is still upon the grass. Many people in England unconsciously long for the return of the Child, for the Kingdom of Heaven here: they work for it, though blindly.

Every time an individual soul surrenders absolutely to the Spirit, and the Christ Child is conceived in him, that desire is closer to fulfilment.

Everyone who bears Christ in his individual life brings closer the time of Peace and Understanding—the time when everyone will realize that man's essential need, even before a "living image," is the need to adore; and to adore through all that he does; so that the first consideration for him in doing his work will be, Does his work increase and restore his likeness to the Creator? does he also make or bring about something in which he sees made manifest the love of goodness that was locked in his heart?

We constantly hear the word "equality," and now reformers, realizing perhaps that equality is something which does not exist in human beings, modify it to "the equality of opportunity"; they fondly imagine that this will give to every man a proper measure of wealth and content.

This is a dream. But there is one equality that is God-given and which governments and dictators cannot give and cannot take away: the equality of desire.

In every man the impulse to desire and pursue his happiness, his own good, is deeply rooted. It is a universal drive and drag towards what is good for him, which dominates every man born.

This equality of desire makes every man search, makes everyone (whether he knows it or not) seek, seek, seek all his life, for the lost Child, whether he knows Him directly as Christ or as the goodness of his human love; as the peace of his home, the joy in his work, or just as the indefinable lightness of heart which descends upon him like Pentecost.

IDOLS

IF, instead of using the expression "spiritual life" we used "the seeking," we should set out from the beginning and go on to the end with a clearer idea of what our life with God will be on this earth; and we should be less vulnerable, that is to say, less easily shattered by disillusionment and discouragement.

"Seek and ye shall find"; that seems to be the quintessence of all spiritual direction for everyone.

Even the saints, who were most conscious of the immanence of God, had to seek during nearly the whole of their lives. Our Lady's own seeking was lifelong, as ours must be. Our Lady experienced this thing largely because it would be our universal experience, and she loved us with Christ's love.

Now we may ask *why* this is so. Why should everyone, saint and sinner, consciously or unconsciously spend most of his life seeking for the lost Child?

To answer that question, there is another which must be answered, and this question is one which we hear asked every day of our lives but very seldom answered.

It is this: How is it that the lives of so many people who profess to be Christian are utterly inconsistent with Christianity?

How is it that people who do not believe in any creed, who have no moral standards and who do not recognize Charity as a thing necessary for salvation, are often conspicuously kind, warm-hearted, and tolerant, whereas professing Christians are notoriously hard, censorious, and exacting?

How is it that a person known to be "religious" is often the very last person to whom we would go with a burden of shame, a problem to be solved, or with our simplest and most constant need for human sympathy?

How is it that so many people who believe that the Charity of Christ fills their hearts as the wind fills the sail of a ship are complacent while people go needy under their own roof?

How is it that Church people give rich and costly vestments to be used at the altar but pass by beggars in the street?

How is it that so many people will send large sums to the missions to convert the unknown heathen, but will go to almost any length to avoid the known borrower, however genuine his need?

How is it that a *great many* people (not only the so-called "over-sensitive") are ashamed to be visibly poor in houses where poverty is preached as an ideal?

How is it that artificial class distinctions are fostered and invested with humiliation in circles that claim the right to teach God's Fatherhood, while in those that deny God, the ideal of Brotherhood repudiates them?

Above all, how is it that those in whom the Holy Spirit—the Spirit of fire and light, truth, beauty, wisdom, and love—abides can so often be narrow, bigoted, timid, mediocre, dull and tepid, impotent in spirit, prudish, detached, suspicious, and careful at the very marriage of heaven and earth?

In Christ's own words, "How is it that thou comest in hither without a wedding garment?"

If we believed that the whole of Christianity consisted in imitating Christ, these extraordinary inconsistencies would be perfectly logical, because it is quite obvious that not one of us, by himself, could imitate Christ: we are a handful of dust, kept together by seventy-five per cent of liquid, with souls that were stained at birth and which are weighted all through our lives with a heavy downward lurch towards sin.

Christ said "Without me you can do nothing," and we see how true this is. How could we imitate an example of uncompromising unworldliness, chastity, sacrifice, and love, offered two thousand years ago by someone we have never seen, when we are unable to keep our promises to people we know well and saw yesterday, and instinctively belittle the qualities of our more heroic friends because we dislike and resent the fact that their example challenges our rationalization of the line of least resistance?

Of course we could but fail if we were merely trying to *imitate* Him.

But that is not what is asked of us, and that is not the meaning of Christianity.

What we *are* asked to do is to be made one with Christ, to allow Him to abide in us, to make His home in us, and gradually, through the oneness that results from living one life, and through the miracles of His love, consummated again and again in Communion with Him, to *become* Christs, to live in Him as Our Lady did. When we are changed into Him as the bread into the Host, then with His power we can follow His example.

This seems to make the question of our inconsistency stranger than ever, because all those inconsistencies are the result of having a misconception of what Christ is like, and it seems almost impossible not to know what someone is like if you share a room with him.

We all know that there is a tendency to skip or skim through those passages in the Gospel which disconcert us, and to form a conception, not only of Christ, but of His special relationship to ourselves, by the passages which are as we say most "consoling" to us.

When I hear Christians discussing economics, I remember a figure who often loomed in my childhood; a very large figure, too, seated squarely and heavily in an armchair on one of the several famous green lawns in her grounds. At her side is a box of sodamint, and a little way behind her back, her acquaintances, whispering—between yawns and within hearing of the child among them taking notes—that her prodigious wealth was derived from the rents of slums. Now this old lady was exacting in piety and a devoted reader of the Bible; whether she ever read any other passages, I do not know, but the passage that she always read to me was the one in which "The Lord is my Shepherd: I shall not want" occurs.

We all tend to that sort of scripture reading. And though we do not depend only on reading, yet it is really necessary, in our search for Christ, to read the Gospel, and to read it all without flinching; or if we must flinch, at least without giving up the attempt.

But we are still faced with the fact that Christ lives with us, in the same room, and we do not know Him.

The Apostles who lived intimately with Him also failed to know Him. What He said to them is just the same thing that He must say to us now: "How long have I been with you and you have not known me?"

It is a fact that very often it is those with whom we live that we know least. It is just as easy to grow to know someone less and less through living in the same room as it is to know him more and more.

This is because we usually judge people by our own reactions, fears, and desires. We do not see them as separate people who possess their own souls and live their own lives, but as part of ourselves and our lives. We attribute to them motives which we would have in the same circumstances.

This is a general tendency, even when we do not share a room. For example, it is almost universally agreed by those who have not got Faith, that all church-goers are insincere and that they only go to church in order to make a good, though false, impression. This would be the critic's own motive, and he is unable to imagine the feelings of someone who has different convictions to his own.

When you share a room it is yet more easy to judge, not only by your own motives, but by your own reactions to all the things that make up daily life, and there is far more constant friction to cause your reactions.

You are tired; you discover that your room-mate is selfish, inconsiderate; she proves it by turning on the radio, banging the door, having a loud voice, and not being tired herself. She is tired; and you are full of well-being; you are irritated to find how selfish she is: gloomy, depressing, a wet-blanket, painfully wanting in moral stamina.

The emotions that are roused by that most unavoidable of things, food, are astonishing. A husband is late for dinner: the first anxiety is for the dinner; then for him; and when he turns up hale and hearty but very late, the wife revenges herself for the pain of anxiety he has caused her by being furious that it was groundless. Now the tragic aspect becomes the spoilt dinner again, and the wife remembers the cooking of it (which she really enjoyed) as hours of abnegation which the brutal man ignores !

We can be totally blinded to the beauty of someone's intellect by his habit of sniffing or blinking which exasperates us.

We can miss more than half of a person's true character by seeing him in a role which some insufficiency of our own demands that he should adopt to us—a protector for example.

Sometimes a really selfish person actually does succeed in making another become just what he wants him to be, no matter how restricted and impoverished the other's life is as a result.

We cannot change Christ; but instead we invent imaginary Christs, and they can be made to be anything at all that we would like Him to be.

Our judgments are always, or nearly always, formed by our own needs and fears and limitations, not by an objective contemplation.

Christ lives in us; but we do not know Him. We form a wrong conception of Him, an ego-projection Christ, an imaginary Christ who fits into our own narrowness, who does not shatter our complacency.

To this imaginary Christ we bring all the fierce zeal and force that is born of the conviction that we are serving God—when we are at least partly serving ourselves —and this is the explanation of the sometimes terrible things we do in good faith, believing that we are serving God.

"The time will come when those who put you to death will think that they do a service to God."

To put it more directly, we build idols.

A moving story is told of a little heathen who was "saved." He edified and delighted the missionaries by his spirit of reverence. He would creep in from the fields and put the flowers he had gathered at the feet of the saints with trembling fingers, then, without lifting his eyes to the carved faces, he would bury his face in his thin golden hands and pray.

He was pointed out to the other children in the orphanage as an example of piety until one day the sister in charge made a shocking discovery.

The devout little convert had made his own private god, an idol roughly carved from the branch of a tree and daubed with vermilion and gold. He had set this up secretly on a pile of stones in a green thicket. Here the sister found it—small, stout, gaudy, and grinning—at its feet the white ash of fires lit in its honour, on its head a crown of little shells. This was, as nearly as poor human hands could make it, the Idol whom the child wanted to adore.

The child wanted a little god that he could hold in his hands; a god who would play with him in the fields; a god with a dark face like his own and clothed in the scarlet and gold that stirred him; a god like himself, limited by his own limitations, and yet one whom he might worship in secret, illimitably. He feared the mild images with pink and white faces and unfamiliar, foreign features.

If he had understood that the one true God is a piccaninny as well as a God; that he is the "black but beautiful" playmate of the little Negro children; that he is the mysterious one who "cometh upon the hills, clothed in dyed garments," the shepherd king in a tunic of scarlet; he would have worshipped and loved Him, and he would not have carved his idol in secret.

We, too, make idols. We make ego-projections of Christ, which are limited to our own narrowness and which justify whatever kind of life we choose to live.

Perhaps "choose" is the wrong word, for many of these life patterns are forced upon us by fear and misunderstanding.

Christ does answer all our real needs. People who have what is called a "special devotion" to one particular aspect of Christ's humanity, find in this approach to Him the true answer to some deep need in themselves.

One of the greatest motives of God's love is to answer the needs of men. Thus, He is a child to the childless, a friend to the friendless, a father to the fatherless, a shepherd to the wanderer, a home to the homeless, a comforter to the mourner, a king to the valiant heart, light to the blind, bread to the hungry, and living water to the thirsty.

If we had kept the strength of our primitive needs, we should not want to make idols. This does not mean if we had remained "savages"; it means that the basic needs, the roots. as it were, of human nature are good; they are given to us by God in His great purpose of increasing life. Love, in its several great manifestations, is given that life may be begotten and nourished and cherished, strengthened and handed on; and not exclusively physical life, but the life of the mind, too. Our other great instinct, self-defence, in its newly created form was just an immense awareness of the wonder of the gift of life, which gave man the instinct to preserve it in gratitude.

But we have let our deep instincts get weak, and twisted them into such false shapes; very often, instead of wanting the contentment of love, we want the satisfaction of lust or of a sense of possessiveness or power. The instinct of self-defence is replaced by fear, a feeling of insufficiency, and a terrible vanity which eats the heart out of us, for the satisfaction which never really satisfies. It is true that sin has twisted these instincts out of shape and set them awry; yet our sacramental life could restore them to their primal innocence.

But we have watered down and whittled away the power of our deepest instincts; we are afraid of the completeness of Love and afraid, or too lacking in vitality, to rejoice fully in the glory of possessing life.

There are people who cannot keep the first commandment because in their heart of hearts they are afraid to keep the second.

They look upon human love as something which competes with the love of God, not as it is—something which completes it.

Their conception of God is no higher than if He were a jealous husband, a man (and the sort of man that few could tolerate and no one could admire).

This in spite of the words of Christ, who said that it is *impossible* to love God and not to love one another, and who implored His followers with His dying breath to love one another.

It is clear that the imaginary Christ these poor people have made in their own minds is exactly opposite to the real Christ.

Our conception of Christ colours our whole life; it informs everything that we touch with its spirit; it makes us what we are.

Nothing could be more untrue than the often-repeated statement that we all worship the same God; or that other, that whatever we worship the result is the same.

Nothing matters more than having a *true* knowledge of Christ.

We become what our conception of Christ is: God made us in His own likeness, but we have an extraordinary power of changing ourselves into the likeness of the idols we make, of those caricatures of God which we set up on the altars of our egoism and worship.

In the degree of the falseness of our conception of God, we restrict and narrow our interests and sympathies; we grow in intolerance and hardness or in a flabbiness which turns to a rot of sweetness like a diabetes of the soul.

In the degree of the truth of our conception of Him, our minds grow broader, deeper, and warmer; our hearts grow wiser and kinder; our humour deeper and more tender; we become more aware of the wonder of life; our senses become more sensitive; our sympathies stronger; our capacity for giving and for receiving greater; our minds are more radiant with a burning light, and the light is the light of Christ.

In the same way that signs and symptoms reveal to us that there is something wrong with our bodies and point to what it is that is wrong, there are psychological signs and symptoms which show us what kind of idol we have made, what kind of false conception of Christ we are confusing with the real one.

One of the commonest symptoms is scruples: the conception of God in the minds (or perhaps I ought to say in the feelings) of scrupulous people is a tragic one.

It is a God who is ever on the lookout to take offence, who is in a continual state of being "grieved."

Not a God with the virility to be really angry, to take drastic action and wipe out the sinner or bring him to book with punishments; but something even worse than that.

Everyone who has suffered from scruples will know what I mean when I say that the mental atmosphere in which they live is like that of a forgotten schoolroom at four o'clock on a dark and foggy winter's day, lit by a low, hissing gas jet, where they sit alone with this tremendous offended God, in an atmosphere permeated by a damp fog of tears.

Even the Passion, in this atmosphere, is misunderstood and becomes something oppressive and frightening which aches in the hearts of the victims of scruples like an open sore.

They have a kind of obsession for the Presence of God, and yet a real shrinking from the thought of Him.

Most of us know how cruel those people who think of themselves as more sensitive than others can be. We know the torture of liking—let alone loving—someone who is always taking offence, who watches us, using his own so-called sensitiveness as a magnifying glass to detect slights and coldness in the smallest involuntary expression on our faces; who has mental ears like whispering galleries, ready to detect hardness of heart in the tones of our voice; who interprets our every action in the twilight of his own obsessional self-pity.

We are unable to maintain friendship with these poor people. The tension in which they force us to live, the nervous self-consciousness they engender in us, becomes unbearable, and if we do not somehow manage to escape (even if it be only through the hardening of our own hearts), we shall become even worse nervous wrecks than they are.

Incredible though it is, people with scruples (excepting some who suffer this trial as part of the world's redemption and by a special grace) have an ego-conception of God which resembles the friend who is continually offended by trifles. In such a presence they are in their own minds condemned to live, and those who are not self-condemned to such a misery cannot imagine the anxiety and depression and fear which drives them to all manner of unkind actions, makes them cowardly and shrinking in all their human relations, and in the end callous to others because they become habitually unaware of what is going on outside the dingy, gas-lit schoolroom of their own souls.

Happily, there are not many people left who have an ego-idol that was frequent not so very long ago: a rigid God, revelling in the letter of the law and only the letter: hard, exacting, and more opposed to pleasure than to sin. But the effect of that idol is still visible in the children of its worshippers, who think themselves to be in revolt against all orthodox religion but who are in fact only remembering the tyranny of their parents' false God.

One very popular idol to-day is the convenient God, the God who (in contrast to those others) is vague, indefinite, ready to wink at the habitual breaking of his laws and to allow his followers to whittle away the purity and splendour and discipline of straight thinking in order to humour their own whims. Indeed, he is almost ready to accept their patronage, for they consider that they are doing him a favour when they pray and that it is he who should be grateful when they go to church.

There are many, many idols, and all of them are revealed by symptoms which must surely stir God's compassion for a poor humanity that devises such torment for itself.

It is easy to see that people become like their conception of God: hard if it is hard; flabby if it is soft; cruel if it is cruel—and I was going to say respectable if it is respectable, but perhaps respectability is not an idol, but simply the Englishman's escape from God.

Now we have one answer to the question, Why must we be always seeking for the lost Child?

Why must we be always feeling the pain of loss?

If we did not, we should not realize that our idols are not God, are not Christ.

Bad as they are, they match our limitations; and if they could content us, we should never know the real beauty of Christ: we should not become whole.

It is one of God's great mercies that, although our vanity and our fear and other mean passions crave for satisfaction, when they *are* satisfied, *we* are not. There is an essential you, an essential me, who cannot be satisfied excepting by God: that is why the sense of loss saves us from complacency in our idols and drives us to go on seeking for the lost Child.

That is why people who seem to have got (and even to have got by their own efforts) all that life can give are so often aware of an inexplicable lack, a want in themselves.

Our conception of Christ makes us what we are, makes our effect on others what it is, influences us and influences everyone with whom we come into contact.

Our Lord said to His Apostles: "It is expedient for you that I go away."

It is the same for us. We know Him only by continually learning Him anew; we get away from false gods only by continually seeking Him; we hold Him only by losing Him.

He goes away from us because it is expedient for us. He goes away that we may seek Him. The sense of loss, the awareness of insufficiency, makes us long for Him as He is; it makes us willing to go out from ourselves and find Him where He is.

He wants us to seek, because He wants to give Himself to us. It is an experience like the experience of emptiness: the emptiness must be there that He may fill it; and we must be aware of it in order that we may want Him to fill it.

"Why hast thou done so to us?"

And the answer is simple, after all: "Seek and ye shall find."

His meaning is Love.

THE LAST CONFESSION

I BROUGHT my flower and flame to the crucifix on the
    wall;
But for the word incarnate not one white star of them
    all,
To Christ the living and dying, crucified in mankind,
Blunt nail in the quick flesh, sharp thorn in the sensitive
    mind.

My candles have burnt out at the carved, archaic feet,
While I passed the poor man by with broken boots in
    the street.
I have said to the worn face of the polished, dark-worn
    wood,
"Lord, Lord!" I was mute to Love's substance in flesh
    and blood!

I have beaten the closed door and asked for a sign from
    God,
While the dry stick in my hand flowered like Aaron's
    rod.
I have strained my mind for a word out of the broken
    cloud,
While Christ stood by and cried from a broken heart
    out loud.

I have been deaf and deaf to the pulse of the heartbeat
Of the dumb women who carry the seed of the world's
    wheat.
Because my neighbour's need has been simple and like my
    own,
Christ, the close friend of the hearth, the known, has
    been unknown.

Lonely sat Love in my house, a stranger under my roof:
Out now my soul and alone, to the stern Judge, the aloof !

PART FOUR

"I will arise now and go about the city in the streets, and
in the broad ways I will seek him whom my soul loveth."
(*Song of Songs*, iii. 2.)

OUR LADY'S SEEKING

MARY and Joseph took the road back to Jerusalem
seeking Christ. They looked for Him, as Mary told
Him, sorrowing. "Thy Father and I have sought thee
sorrowing."

If you have ever loved anyone very deeply and then
lost him through separation, estrangement, or even by
death, you will know that there is an instinct to look for
him in every crowd.

The human heart is not reasonable; it will go on seeking for those whom it loves even when they are dead.
It will miss a beat when someone passes by who bears
them the least resemblance: a tilt of the hat, an uneven
walk, a note in the voice.

When St. Augustine was a boy he lost his dearest
friend, and he had to leave the town where they had
lived together because it became an obsession with him,
this looking for the faintest likeness to the dead friend
in the crowds thronging the streets that he had once
walked in.

Mary and Joseph must have looked into every face
of those crowds streaming out of Jerusalem, with
even more hunger and sorrow than the heartbroken
Augustine.

Sometimes it occurs to one, when some friend has
been dead for years: "Would I know him now, suppose he did come back? Is there not just the possibility
that I might pass him in the crowd without recognizing
him?"

It is less fantastic than it sounds, for sometimes we do in fact remember people's personalities and forget their faces.

There would have been no doubt whatever of Our Lady's knowing her son's face; but often, in the dusk, she must have searched for it in the face of another boy, and the boy would have wondered who this woman was and why she leaned down and searched his face; he could not have guessed that the day would come when the Mother of God would really find her son in every boy and every boy would be able to give Christ back to her.

Her search did not end when she found Him in the Temple, and it did not really begin when she lost Him on the road from Jerusalem.

From the hour when Gabriel saluted her, the little girl in Nazareth, she had had to seek for Him through faith: to believe that he was in her; to believe that this little child whom she rocked to sleep was God; that it was God whom she taught to walk, to speak, to hold a spoon.

After the finding in the Temple He returned to Nazareth and was obedient to her and Joseph. She had to believe that it was God who obeyed them; God who grew and who increased in wisdom.

Later on, she was again seeking for Christ, this time among the crowd that thronged round Him in His public life. She is among those who are trying to get close to Him: therefore, she is among the sick, the crippled, the blind, the poorest beggars—outcasts of every description. For such are the people who follow Christ in every age.

It is just like Our Lady, this: she, who did not seek an exalted or solitary life in which to prepare for Christ's birth, is content now to follow Him in the crowd, to seek Him among strangers in the public street.

In our days there is very little solitude for those who really try to get close to Christ in the world, who want to prove the sincerity of their love by taking their share of the burden on the back of humanity. Like Our Lady they must come to Him in the crowds.

So it is with the soldier in his camp, the airman at his post, the sailor in his ship, the fireman at his station.

So it is with the hospital nurse, the factory worker, and the government servants in the huge departments. So it is with the refugees driven together on the roads and to the communal living of the homeless; so also with the people in the shelters and in all the circumstances of war. True to her consistent compassion for us, her entering into our experience, the few glimpses that we have of Our Lady nearly all show her in the crowd: crowded out of the inns at Bethlehem, when Christ was born; seeking Him in the crowds on the road back to Jerusalem; persuading Him to His first miracle at a crowded marriage feast; seeking Him in the crowd in His public life. Even in the immense loneliness on Calvary she was surrounded by the crowd around the Cross.

She had followed this crowd to Calvary, but while most of the people stood a little way off, to mock, to stare, to become hysterical with blood lust and the hatred of goodness—some perhaps to mourn for Him, but at a little distance—she passed through them at last, and at last came close to Him.

She stood at the foot of the Cross: not to mourn—that would have been far too small, far too remote from Him, for the sharing in the Passion which was her part—she came there to die—to stand quietly by the Cross and die.

The first great finding was in the Temple.

The second great finding was on Calvary.

"Did you not know that I must be about my Father's business?"

"Father, I have finished the work that you gave me to do."

Mary found her lost Child on Calvary.

The condition of finding Him was the loss of herself. *She* had to die, even out of her self-donation to God. Self had to die out of her love, and this in spite of the fact that self in her was not egoism but simply the *being*: the separate being of herself which made it possible for her to do the will of God with her own will.

In our love, self becomes selfishness. In Our Lady it was a flawless self-giving.

Her unity with Christ was complete: they were one.

He sacrificed His life: life died in Life itself.

Because He sacrificed Himself, she had to sacrifice herself: she was sacrificed *in Him*.

Her blameless selfhood had to die out of her love, simply because it was Christ, and Christ chose to die.

On Calvary she saw herself die in Christ.

She had seen her flesh and blood, her life, born in Christ, when she held Him between her hands shivering at the first touch of the night air.

She wrapped Him in swaddling bands and laid Him in a manger.

Now she saw her flesh and blood, her life, dead in Christ, when she held Him between her hands, frozen by the first touch of death.

She wrapped Him in swaddling bands and laid Him in the tomb.

Now there was another three days' loss, dark and empty as those in which she had sought for Him sorrowing.

Like Christ, she had turned her face "steadfastly towards Jerusalem" on that day years ago: like Him, she never looked back.

It had been enough for her to follow the path marked out by His footprints. She did not ask where they would lead her. In the end they were scored in crimson and led to the Cross. With illimitable courage, she trod all the way in them.

Now He was laid in the tomb, but she had found the lost Child.

When Christ saw her standing by His Cross and near her the boy apostle, John, He said to her: "Woman, behold thy son."

There can be no doubt about His meaning.

A few hours earlier, this boy had sat at table with Christ. He had leaned his head upon Christ's breast and heard His heart beating. And that heartbeat was the music accompanying His prayer, the prayer offered on what was very nearly His last breath.

He prayed that all those who loved Him should be made one with Him, that they should all live in Him, so that they would have only one life: His.

This oneness with Him for which Christ prayed was more real, more complete, than anything we can imagine, or experience in any other way. It includes every kind of human oneness but exceeds them all.

Just listen to His own description of it: "As thou, Father, in me and I in thee."

The oneness of God.

From the moment when Christ told Our Lady to see Him, her son, in John, she saw Christ in all Christians. She took her only son to her heart in all men born.

She saw now but one Man abiding in mankind.

How far from her would it have been to say that because she loved Christ, she could love no one else: she knew the secret: there *was* no one else.

As He looked down from the Cross, with eyes already full of death, Christ saw a huge crowd of people around Him. For these people He was dying. Yet He did not say to Mary:

"Mother, behold me in this crowd." Or: "Mother, take me to your heart in humanity." For to Him, as to His Father, each *one* in the crowd was present, and He loved each *one* as if that one alone existed. It was not for a crowd that He was dying, but for each person in the crowd; not for the human race, but for each member of the human race.

Those reformers who think that men can be made to love one another by legislation, that the Kingdom of Heaven can be provided by the county council, that the brotherhood of man can exist without the Fatherhood of God, always have in their minds a picture of a multitude, which they call "humanity."

But no one can serve humanity, can make men happy, unless he first knows one man, unless he knows what spells happiness for one man, what things are to one man's peace.

In the face of a multitude—real or imaginary—it is easy to forget the needs of each one in the multitude. Face to face with one man, we cannot forget, we cannot fail to know, what he wants and what he needs. For he has a life like our own, woven of joys and sorrows, anxieties and fears, work and loves. He has a wife and children, or else the problem of living without them. He needs to think, to learn, to have poetry in his life; to see an inward meaning in the things of every day. He needs faith and sacraments; he needs some explanation of suffering; he needs wise guidance and education to help him to grasp the truth of justice; he needs sympathy, stimulus for courage; he needs work which will not only bring in the food for his body but will content his soul and will be the means by which his likeness to the Trinity can be restored to him. He needs a reasonable measure of solitude, and he has the right to the secrets of his own soul, the right to set his own standard, to suffer his own sorrows; and, above all, he has the right, the necessity, and the obligation to adore.

All this can be forgotten and left out when one thinks in terms of "humanity," but face to face with one man it cannot be forgotten.

Before God there is one Man, Christ.

Humanity is as many times one man as there are people in the world.

Our Lady took all men to herself in John, this one human being in whom Christ dwelt.

Once again Christ was forming in Mary, for the Advent had come which was her preparation for bearing Christ in all the Christians in the world. And, just as in the first Advent, she served Him by serving another man. Then it was Joseph; now it was John.

Until Christ became man, her story was inaudible, inaudible until He laughed and spoke and wept: when His voice was heard on earth no more, Mary too returned to silence.

It was the silence and obscurity of ordinariness, of her extraordinary humility; and once again it was our life.

It was another Advent, a withdrawing and folding upon the Life within her life; but a withdrawing that did not separate her from other people but only brought her closer to them; for she had found her Christ in them all.

She found Christ in everyone, and everyone found Christ in her, because they did not know that she was an extraordinary person who had given birth to God or that she had given birth to a mysterious life in themselves. They only knew that she was inexhaustibly sympathetic, illimitably wise, and wholly lovable.

At Pentecost she was with the Apostles, and the Spirit descended upon them and filled the earth with His glory. The Bride of the Spirit heard the silence of her own heart singing.

OUR SEEKING

IN our seeking for the lost Child, our contemplation of Our Lady becomes active.

The *fiat* was complete surrender.

Advent was a folding upon the life growing in our darkness.

Now the seeking is a going out from ourselves.

It is a going out from our illusions, our limitations, our wishful thinking, our self-loving, and the self in our love.

Yet this outgoing begins gently: it has something of the quality of Advent. Before the Divine Child leaves us, we are allowed to experience the loveliness of His indwelling presence; therefore, when he has gone, the longing to find Him again will be stronger than anything we may meet in the seeking; stronger than the fear which makes us want to remain locked up in our own limitations. No matter how hard the way, it will be in some measure sweet to us, and we shall take it, not as a path along which we are driven, but as one whose attraction we cannot resist, because we know that on it we shall some day discover Him.

Where must we seek?

Everywhere—in everyone.

How must we seek?

With faith and courage and limitless love.

First of all, by faith.

Faith is something immeasurably more than a sixth sense, more than intuition, more than feeling or knowledge.

It not only enables us to believe in the miracles which throng our lives, but it makes our charity a thousand times more sensitive.

With faith we are like blind people learning, through the touch of caressing fingers, the features of the face that we cannot see. We discover the Face that we seek in every human face; and just because we must seek with a more sensitive medium than sight, we are not put off by the visible things: the mutilation, bruises, sweat, dirt, and tears. Beyond all this we discern the invisible beauty of the Man abiding in mankind. It is in faith that we discover the lost Child.

Our Lady must have had to make her act of faith in Advent.

Surely she would not have believed that God was a child in her womb, had He not said so!

That is what faith is: believing something because God has told us that it is so.

It is not believing something because we feel that it is true or because we want it to be true or because our reason can encircle it. Truth would be a very small and petty thing if it would fit into our minds.

If we took the sum-total of all our moods, how seldom, if ever, would we be convinced by them that the Holy Spirit is within us and wishes to be at home in us. This is too mysterious a thing for us to accept through anything less than the word of God Himself.

We begin our seeking by making acts of faith in the presence of Christ in our own souls.

Our Lady must have helped to form Christ in her soul by making acts of faith in His hidden presence within her.

Sometimes, when she sat down in the cottage doorway after her day's work, she must have felt anew her amazement at the angel's salutation and have asked her own soul:

"How can this thing be?" Could it be possible that the tiny little tunic that she was weaving was for *God*?

That she had to guess the tiny size of God by the measure of her own littleness?

"How can this thing be?"

Acts of faith in the presence of Christ in us are the first active exercise in this contemplation.

It is quite incredible to think that God is really present in me.

"My God, I believe that you are within me."

This act of faith brings peace: it silences the noise of distraction, the loud business of fear.

It is the stilling of the waters.

It gathers our thoughts into a circle like a crown of flowers; it crowns us with peace.

As to the vanities, anxieties, scruples, and all the other distractions, we can let them pass over us like a dark wave passing over a swimmer, and pay no heed to them.

Christ our Lord is within us; there is no room for any other awareness; everything that we see and touch and taste and think must be related to this one fact.

We can copy His Mother and clothe Him in our

thoughts, lay them upon Him like garments: a tiny shift of white linen and a little crimson surcoat, thoughts that the belief in His presence make radiant with purity and love.

We can make Him a child's crown with the daisies that grow in our fields: and since He, who is timeless, is with us in time, we will fetch Him a thistledown clock, one of the coltsfoot flowers that grow in the ruins of our bombed cities.

Because He is in the little house of our being, we will learn to control our minds, to gather our thoughts to silence, and to crown them with peace, just as we learn to control our voices and to move softly when a child is asleep in the house of bricks and mortar.

We know by faith that Christ is in our own family; it is He whom we foster in our children. When you tell your child a story, when you play a game with your little son, you tell a story, you play a game with the Christ Child.

One of our commonest natural experiences of the sense of loss is tiredness: it empties us out; it is almost as if we had let the infant fall from our hands.

It is useless to flog a tired mind, useless to reproach a tired heart; the only way to God, when we are tired out, is the simplest wordless act of faith.

A woman too weary for articulate prayer will find that for her the best of all prayer is the unspoken act of faith in Christ in her children. When she knows that she is setting the table and baking the cake for the Christ Child, her soul will be at rest.

When Our Lady's little boy tumbled and grazed his knees, what acts of faith she must have made as she bathed them—faith like that which enabled her to believe, when she saw the Son of God fall beneath the Cross and could not pick Him up.

Awareness of the presence of the Divine Child in us draws us off from every distracting and destructive pre-occupation, such as self-pity, anxiety, irritability with other people, the morbidity which leads us to dwell more upon our own sinfulness than upon the beauty of God.

In the wonder of this awareness, we are able to accept the humiliation of being ourselves.

The next act of faith is in Christ in other people.

It is very easy to believe in the indwelling presence of Christ in the souls of imaginary people; to believe in it in people whom we do not know; but it is very difficult to believe in it in the case of our own relations and our intimate friends.

Somehow it is difficult to believe that the Holy Spirit abides in people who are not picturesque. When we think of Christ in the workman, we think of Him in a special kind of workman who wears an open shirt and is assisted in carrying the burden of social injustice by a truly magnificent physique. We do not think of Him in the man who delivers the milk or calls to mend the pipes. We do not think of Him in the porters in the apartment houses. Recently, in a big block, a frail little porter fell down dead. Everyone agreed that the heavy luggage he had been in the habit of carrying for the tenants was too much for him, though only after a post mortem was it realized. No one was struck by the idea that in this little man a scene from the Passion had been lived again; he had fallen under the weight of the Cross.

It is easy to believe in Christ in the refugee when he is on the road, easy to believe when the refugee mother arrives at an English port, with a shawl round her head and a baby in her arms; but how hard to believe in the presence of God in the same refugees when they have got good work, are housed and fed, and possess hats and gloves.

They must be quite without vision who are not reminded of the flight into Egypt by the road from Dunkirk; but we are all apt to forget that the Holy Family lived in Egypt for a time and must have got work and lodging and been glad of friends; and there must have been some who looked upon them with the incredible suspicion that every race has for foreigners when the foreigners become independent.

Just as we cannot depend upon feelings to know that Christ is in ourselves, we cannot depend upon appearances to know that He is in others.

That which is true of the Host is true of people. We cannot discern God's presence through our senses, but faith tells us that we should treat one another with the reverence that we give to the Host.

We need to bring to other people faith like that which we bring to the Blessed Sacrament.

It is really as easy to believe in one as in the other. We have exactly the same reason for believing in both: the word of Christ.

Both are miracles of love which, like God's peace, pass understanding.

We have no difficulty in believing that Christ is in us when we receive Holy Communion, or that He is in all the others who come up to the altar rails, from the old Chelsea pensioner in his red coat to the child of seven, opening his mouth like a fledgling for his ration of heaven.

We believe easily in the presence of Christ in the Host, because it is an idea with which we are familiar. We have made daily acts of faith in it, and we accept it easily.

If we made daily acts of faith in the presence of Christ in other people, we should soon accept that, too. It would be the first step in discovering the lost Child.

An old man whose love for his fellow creatures endeared him to them all confessed that whomsoever he met —before greeting him out loud—he greeted Christ within him in secret.

Such a practice as that, begun darkly in faith, would soon teach us to believe, too, just as genuflecting before the tabernacle teaches babies to believe that God is "in there."

Faith simplifies the search. We do not have to discover in which of several people Christ is to be found: we must look for Him in them all. And not in an experimental spirit, to discover *whether* He is in them or not, but with the absolute certainty that He *is*.

Christ does not choose to be known through outward appearances—even the appearance of virtue.

The way in which we get to know Christ in others through faith is akin to the way in which we get to know something indefinable in others through affection: the "something" which makes them themselves.

As we become more and more continually aware of that "something," it becomes our most real consciousness of them, and we become less conscious of their outward appearances, their faces and their bodies. Also, our own attitude to people changes their appearance in our eyes. People when we first meet them, do not look at all as they will look when we know them well.

Anyone who has ever been on a journey by sea, or even to a new school, knows that on the first day we are astonished to see how queer everyone around us looks; but if, at the end of the journey or of the first term, someone new came along and remarked the same queerness, we should be most indignant.

If we look for Christ only in the saints, we shall miss Him. If we look for Him only in those people who seem to have the sort of character we personally consider to be Christian, that which we call our "ideal," we shall miss the whole meaning of His abiding in us.

If we look for Him in ourselves, in what we imagine to be the good in us, we shall begin in presumption and end in despair.

Our search through faith and courage and love is a great going out into darkness, a reaching out to others in darkness, believing that Christ is there in each one; but not in the way that we expect, not in the way that we think He should be, not in the way that we already

understand, but in the way that He chooses to be,
Who is Himself the Way.

"He is higher than heaven and what wilt thou do?
He is deeper than hell and how wilt thou know?"

The meaning of the Mystical Body of Christ is that
Christ lives in all Christians. The practical result of this,
for us, is that now on earth the whole of Christ's life is
always being lived; the things that happened to Him on
earth are happening to Him now in His members. The
things that He did on earth He is doing now through us.
In us are all His needs as man: His need of food and
drink and sleep; of sympathy, friendship, comfort, and
love; His need of solitude, His need to adore.

No single one of us can lead all of His life; to do so
would be to live all the lives of all the people who live
now, who ever have lived, and who ever will live. He did
live all men's lives in His one life, because there is no
limit at all to His capacity: but our capacity is very limited
indeed. The experience of even one human emotion is
sharply restricted in us by the narrowness of our hearts.
Even a child, whose capacity is so much bigger than that
of a grown-up person, soon falls asleep, worn out, if
he is visited by great joy or grief, and it is a matter of
every day to see a child laugh while tears are wet on his
cheeks.

Each one of us can only live a fragment of Christ's life
at one time, perhaps one moment of it or one incident or
one experience. But through our communion with one
another in Him, through our oneness with one another
because of His one life in us all, we make up what is
wanting in one another and are whole; and in us all, as
one Body, His whole life is lived.

Because He is not limited but is illimitable Love, His
joy and sorrow go on forever: the temptation in the
wilderness; the delight in the fields of corn and the birds
and the wild flowers; His need for other people's response
to Him; His ardent joy in giving us the Sacred Host; and
many other things which, as St. John says, would fill all

the books in the world if they were written, go on in us through all time.

There are two aspects of this mystery. One is that we have Christ's power to give: He has given us, so to speak, His own will and hands and heart. The other is that we have His power to receive.

We can accept in His power. This accepting is as much a part of our Christ-life as giving in His name. The need that cries out in us is His need, and just as we are to be "other Christs" to our friends, *they* are to be "other Christs" to us: in giving to us, they, too, are to know the joy of His bestowing. We may not deny it to them. This interchange and interlocking of Christ's love should be a continual communion between us.

The pride which wants to give but not to receive, which resents sympathy and is content with unrequited love, is terrible, because it is pride which frustrates Christ. Where would we be, poor human creatures, were it not that Christ pleads from every human life, a beggar with outstretched hands?

In every one of us there is some lack which is Christ's need. It makes it possible for all of us to give to Him, through the limited means that we have. It is the courtesy of God, Who gives us His good measure, pressed down, shaken together and running over, and is not only content, but is even grateful, for our little pipkin of love in return.

When Our Lady found her son in the Temple at Jerusalem, she asked Him why He had submitted her and Joseph to this search.

He answered, "Did you not know that I must be about my Father's business?"

That answers us when we ask the same question, and it answers the question: Why does Christ hide His glory and manifest Himself in humility, poverty, and necessity?

It is because He must be about His Father's business. His Father's business, the purpose of His life in human creatures, is to love and be loved.

That is the reason of our being in God; that is the reason of Christ's abiding in us. That is His sole purpose in man, to love and be loved.

Therefore Christ wants to be accessible: He wants to be disarmed of His glory so that the inglorious can come to Him without fear, so that He may come to the lowliest and least and be taken to their hearts.

For the same reason, He made the Host of the simplest of materials, unleavened bread, so little and light, so easy of access.

God's purpose is love; how to win the human heart, how to give it life.

There could not be a more ingenious way than the one He has devised, His way of hiding Himself in us, revealing His presence in our necessities, so that we can only find him by obeying His commandment: "Little children, love one another!"

He hides and can be found, not only in a child, but in your child; not only in a friend, but in your friend; not only in a servant, but in your servant: could there be easier access to Him than your child, your friend, your servant?

We do not love people because we admire them or because they are "honest, sober and respectable." In fact, poor things that we are, we are chilled by the sight of too much righteousness, too many virtues in which we feel unable to share. We do not love people because they are beautiful or clever. We do not love people because they are efficient or well dressed. Indeed, love is more likely to grow out of our being at ease with people, and most of us are more likely to be at ease with those who are shabby and fallible. We do not love people because they are witty, although we will put up with a great deal to be amused, even by people who have tongues like little whips, or a gift for mimicry which we feel sure will raise a laugh at our own expense as soon as our backs are turned. We do not love people for any of these things; and though we may admire them and enjoy them briefly, they do not induce us to remain and perhaps to grow into love through intimacy.

It is impossible to define exactly why we love when we do, but it is easy to point to those things which do compel us to remain with certain people and from which love almost certainly results.

They are: fellow feeling; shared difficulties; knowing that something is wanted which it is in our power to give; knowing ourselves to be needed; doing the same work; facing the same perils; enduring the same hardships—such things provide the soil in which love can take root.

Probably the British people not only expressed, but really experienced, more kindness and goodness to one another during the bombing of Britain than ever before. The intensity of the friendships between soldiers is well known.

Love is most likely of all to spring from another's need of us, and the fact of spending ourselves for another always generates new life in us.

Everyone who has nursed the sick or wounded knows that for so long as the patient needs it, a special grace of life-giving energy is given to the nurse. To give life is the purpose of love, and we love those people most of all whose needs waken a response in us that floods us with creative energy, causing us to put out new green shoots of life.

The same work, the same needs, the same perils, the same temptations, the same poverty: these are the things which attract, compel, and hold us; from them springs the love that gives life. Therefore Christ manifests Himself to us in just these things.

It is very often the response in ourselves that tells us that we have found the lost Child, that one of those glimpses of Him which sweeten life has been vouchsafed to us. Usually, it is not by anything outward that we recognize Him, but by a sudden rush and sweetness of life within us like the quickening of the unborn St. John the Baptist, when he recognized the unborn Christ in Mary's womb.

Thus it is that when we find Him in others we also find Him in ourselves.

If Our Lady's innocent selfhood had to die in her Son's dying for us; if we are sincere, that is to say, if our true object in this contemplation of Our Lady is to be united with God; then it is certain that the self must die in our love: not the love itself—never that—but the selfishness in it.

This happens in many different ways, and no one should be afraid. Sometimes it is a gentle process; sometimes it is the Kingdom of Heaven suffering violence; but however it happens, we are given grace for it by that same infinitely tender Father who cherishes even the cheeky little sparrows hopping in the London gutters.

The giving up of our own idea of how Christ should be in another person is one way of sifting the chaff out of our love and purifying it. This is the way for the idealist. The demand that someone we love should conform to our ideal is often unjust and cruel. There is pride in it, too. "She whom I love (or who loves me) must be thus and thus"—how unlike the lovely humility of the poet who sang:

> " And human love needs human meriting:
>   How hast thou merited—
> Of all man's clotted clay the dingiest clot ?
>   Alack, thou knowest not
> How little worthy of any love thou art ! "

How shocking is the sentence that we so often hear in the plaintive voice of self-pity: "I did all I could to *make* him happy." Who has not met the head of the family who orders a "command" pleasure and punishes his children if they do not enjoy it.

There is possessiveness in the idealist's attitude. Unconsciously, he is saying: "You are to be like me. I will shape you, or hammer you, into the shape of my ideal. You must enjoy my pleasures. Your tastes must coincide with mine. You must have only my values. You must be restricted by my limitations."

This attitude, when it is allowed to go unchecked, can reach terrible proportions. From the individual, it passes to the group. Certain schools, youth groups, and political organizations make it a boast that they produce a certain "type."

This attitude is only possible when one person regards another as his property—"mine," body and soul. The totalitarian state says: "Everyone in this country is to be as I want him to be or perish." And soon this is changed to "everyone in the world."

There is a very strong tendency in the world to-day to want Christianity to be smooth, attractive, respected by everyone, powerful in the world's sense; but now, as long ago, Christ remains on the Cross.

The dying of self in the idealist's love should lead not to cynicism but to the discovery of Christ in need of him. Our Lady loved Him in His defeat and disfigurement, since this was His choice. Her attitude is the one in which the healing of the pride of totalitarianism begins. And just as this healing began in her, it can begin in us now, when we respect a friend's right to be himself and look beyond our own egoism for the showing of Christ in him.

In a world like ours in which, for so long, marriage has been treated lightly, there are bound to be a very great number of difficult tangled relationships, and many people must have their selves dying through a real crucifixion of their love. It is often very hard. So much so that, in spite of many other reasons which they offer for being outside the Church, the real reason that keeps a multitude out is a cherished, illicit love. This, and the death of someone loved, is crucifixion, and we have to pray, in the words of Paul Claudel, that God will have pity "On husband and wife betrayed; son, mother, death shall part; And on him who must needs tear a passionate love from his heart."

Those who share in Our Lady's courage will be comforted for the deaths of their sons if, as she did with St. John, they take the youth of the world to their hearts as their responsibility; and foster in those who are growing up to inherit the countries that their sons died to save, that same Christhood which was the flower of their own boys' lives and gave them the courage to die.

When those mothers find Christ in the children growing up in the world, in a mysterious way they will discover their own lost sons again.

There are as many ways in which self can die out of our love as there are loves in the world, but there is one which we need to think of very much to-day: forgiveness. It is strange to say that we discover Christ in one another by forgiving one another. Perhaps this is because we have a wrong conception of forgiveness. So often, alas, as we use it, it is condescension following upon condemnation. But it should not be. It should be the most direct way of healing a wound. It goes beyond all possible explanations and all possible misunderstandings. It does not even ask to be understood.

Nothing could work more against the discovery of the lost Child in another than to foster bitterness against someone we love or to have an enemy.

Christ is utterly sinless; if someone has injured us, it cannot be the Christ in him that has injured us. But no one can do a wrong without wounding himself. Sin always wounds the sinner, but Christ has taken this great wounding to Himself. All His wounds, all His suffering, the whole of His passion, is the wounding of sin—ours the sinning; His the redeeming wound of our sin.

Forgiveness, then, is a reaching out to comfort and heal that wound in our friend which Christ in him bears because of the wrong he did to us: to forgive is to ask Christ to forgive us. "Forgive and you shall be forgiven."

So, too, to be forgiven. When we ask and give forgiveness, we discover Christ's redeeming wounds in one another. And when we ask the Father to forgive us, He discovers the Child who was lost in us. He sees the shining wounds of Mary's Son, the lost Child in the human race come back to Him. And God forgives.

THE WAY

WE do not see the purpose of certain things; particularly such things as frustration.

Why was this child born half-witted?

Why did that young man die?

Why has that brilliant scholar been suddenly blinded?

Why does that sick old woman, who has outlived all who loved her, linger on in her misery?

These questions and countless others could easily be answered if we could realize the extraordinary humility and tenderness in which Christ approaches the human heart.

If we understood the courtesy of God, we should not be scandalized by the grief of the world: not, indeed, that God has caused all these evils, or that He wills them, but that He has hallowed them.

He could have approached us through beauty and power and strength, but He has chosen to come to us through littleness and humility; and for His great purpose, the lives that we consider the most useless are often the best material.

In our lifelong seeking for the lost Child, how shall we recognize Him?

The beginning of recognition will consist in knowing what sort of thing to expect.

If only we could read the Gospels with a completely new mind and without baulking at the parts which disconcert us, it would be easier to recognize the same Christ doing the same things now.

Very few people read the whole of the Gospels without shying at something, but to read them whole is one of the essential steps in seeking for the lost Child.

Unless we do read the Gospels honestly we cannot know what He is like, and who can seek for someone whom they would not recognize if they found him?

The Gospel is the touchstone of recognition.

In the very beginning of it there is a lesson in how to seek for the lost Child. He is the Light of the world. The idea of light floods the Gospels. It seems that it has always been impossible to think of God without the idea of light filling the mind.

By the light of a star, the first who sought for Him, after Mary, were guided. They followed a star, seeking the light of the world, expecting to find a newly born king, someone visibly predestined to be a great leader. They found a peasant's new-born baby in a stable. and they worshipped Him.

Christ is the Light of the World; the sun which shines upon everything; gives colour to everything; heals and gives life, light, and heat; the warmth that goes down deep to the root of the tree and discovers the tiniest seedling in the darkness and feeds it and draws it up into the day. But it is not only as the light of the sun that Christ wishes to be seen, but also as the little candle burning in the house, a candle in a dark room.

"I am the Way," He said. And when we read the Gospels we begin to recognize what this means to those who are seeking for Him in human beings. For everywhere, in everyone, there is some moment or experience of His going on, all through time. On earth He was little, joyful, afraid, sorrowful, tempted, loving, a failure, a king —everything that we can be, excepting a sinner; and even in sinners He is there in the Tomb, lying dead, awaiting and desiring resurrection.

All the ages of Christ on earth must be continually manifest in men: infancy, babyhood, boyhood, adolescence, manhood; also the life in the womb, the three days dead, the risen life, and the life in the Host.

All His actions; His healing, pity, teaching, fasting, weeping, praying, giving.

In some people one aspect, even one moment of Christ's life, continues always, or comes back again and again.

In some, different aspects occur: they pass from one experience to another. Some are always in His childhood; others experience His Passion. Even children experience His Passion, for our natural age has very little to do with our Christ-age, and the fact of being in Christ at all implies a state of childhood in the soul, a child's almost infinite capacity for experiencing joy and sorrow completely.

Moments in the Gospel occur in moments of people's lives now, and throw a light upon the whole meaning of that life for us.

A young priest was celebrating his first Mass. In the front of the church his mother and his young brothers knelt. It was easy to know them by their likeness to him —a family of dark, golden-skinned boys, and the mother like them.

When the Mass was ended, and the new priest came back into the sanctuary for the blessing and the kissing of the consecrated hands, the family hesitated shyly, almost paralysed by wonder and love; and before they could go first (as they should have done) to the altar rails, the crowd had pushed past them, strangers had taken their place. The faithful were flocking around their new shepherd, and his mother and his brother had become part of the crowd, waiting their turn until the end

For one moment the young priest looked over the bowed heads into his mother's eyes, and his face shone.

"My mother and my brethren are they who hear the word of God and do it."

Because the priesthood had made him the Christ of the people, he belonged to them; he was their kith and kin, their son and brother, *their* Christ, the priest at the altar.

People often seem to think of Our Lady as aggrieved, slighted, when this happened to her !

I think she and her Son looked across the heads of the crowds to one another with just that understanding and gratitude that shone on the faces of the young priest and his mother, and Christ's words on that occasion were spoken to Mary and in thanksgiving.

Only Our Lady has ever lived all the aspects and phases and moments of Christ completely.

In some He is newly born.

In some He is a child.

In some He is homeless.

In some He is ignored, unrecognized, mocked, betrayed.

In some He is hungry; in some He is naked; in some He is helpless.

Here are examples, but they are not exhaustive: indeed, they are only hints at the countless manifestations of Christ in man.

First, Christ adoring, through the contemplatives who pray day and night, singing and saying the offices of the Church: Christ remains on earth adoring His Father.

He remains on earth unrecognized, chiefly in the saints. For though, when they are dead, men see their glory and bring their little candles to burn palely in it, like flames in sunlight, while they live they are seldom known for what they are, and are usually thought to be eccentric, ridiculous, even positively hypocritical. To their families, they are generally a nuisance; to the many good people who are unconsciously ashamed of being religious and try to represent religion as *only* sociology or *only* reformed economic conditions, the saints are a rebuke and challenge hardly to be suffered, for their way is always the impractical way of the Sermon on the Mount: poverty, humility, the folly of the Cross. And yet, when the years move on and we look back, we find that it is not the social reformer or the economist or even the church leader who has done tremendous things for the human race, but the silly saints in their rags and tatters, with their empty pockets and their impossible dreams. It is the saints who made universities and hospitals and schools, the saints who fought against slavery, who saved children abandoned by their parents, who went out and tended lepers, who taught the poor; a saint who anticipated the Red Cross.

Christ remains a child on earth—not only in actual children but in helpless people, in simple-minded people, and in the many moments of simplicity that come to the sophisticated.

In the dying, He is nearly always a child. Anyone who has seen death often, will tell you that it is common for the dying to go back in their minds to their childhood; very often, as they die, they are little children again, calling to their mothers to come to them in this strange darkness; thus it is that many fulfil the condition for entering the Kingdom of Heaven, suffering their desolation with the child's undiluted capacity for suffering but with death robbed of its terror by the child's capacity for perfect trust.

The Child Christ lives on from generation to generation in the poets, very often the frailest of men but men whose frailty is redeemed by a child's unworldliness, by a child's delight in loveliness, by the spirit of wonder.

Christ was a poet, and all through His life the Child remains perfect in Him. It was the poet, the unworldly poet, who was King of the invisible kingdom; the priests and rulers could not understand that. The poets understand it, and they, too, are kings of the invisible kingdom, vassal kings of the Lord of Love, and their crowns are crowns of thorns indeed.

He remains, being tempted in all those who are

tempted: in those who are in mortal sin, He is in the tomb.

We should never come to a sinner without the reverence that we would take to the Holy Sepulchre.

Pilgrims have travelled on foot for years to kiss the Holy Sepulchre, which is empty. In sinners we can kneel at the tomb in which the dead Christ lies.

Christ is in Gethsemane in all those who are crushed by fear, by shame, by the sense of guilt, by the neurotic type of scruple, by the sensitive awareness of the tragedy of the world and of sin as its cause. He is present in all those who are afraid of the sacrifice asked of them and who seek help and sympathy and the prayers of others.

The incidents of His life are reproduced over and over again in innumerable ways.

For example, His falling under the Cross.

He is under the heavy Cross in those who have fallen under the load of debt, loneliness, shame, hardship, temptation. Those who feel secure, who do not know what it is to stagger under a burden of temptation or bitter circumstance, cannot see Christ under the Cross to-day; but for the others, the afflicted, those who are conscious of their own weakness when something must be borne, here is a grace indeed: they can share the shame or trouble, pay the debt, make reparation for the sin, lift the Cross from Christ, be Simon of Cyrene to Him.

There is the stripping of the garments.

In so many diverse ways, Christ is stripped of His garments. In the recruits and conscripts, literally stripped naked by the soldiers as Christ was.

In the new soldier who breaks down and weeps for his wife and children before the others.

In the people whose homes have been bombed and who have lost all they had and all that made home.

In the people who have been found out in some shameful thing, not only before the world—which in extremes like this matters little—but before the one person whose faith in them *was* their world.

In school children, exposed in the pathetic lies of wishful fantasy to which their starved emotions compelled them and which neither they nor their mocking classmates understand.

In the old nurse whose charge has outgrown her, and who, for the fourth or fifth time, must go away with her frustrated motherhood exposed and appearing absurd.

In the woman who had only her youth and her comeliness, suddenly stripped of it all by a stroke or disfiguring illness.

In the late convert who must strip off habit after habit of indulgence that adheres to his will like a garment adhering to an open wound.

In the lover who, with his own hands, has laid his heart bare and shown all the subtlest tenderness of his sensitive mind and all the holy secret of himself, only to be scorned or met with indifference. Is not he Christ stripped of His garments? All that is holy looks absurd; all that is beautiful looks ugly: all that is secret is violated. He stands and bleeds.

In many people Christ lives the life of the Host. Our life is a sacramental life.

This Host life is like the Advent life, like the life of the Child in the womb, the Child in the swaddling bands, the Christ in the tomb. It is a life of dependence upon creatures, of silence and secrecy, of hidden light. It is the life of a prisoner.

The Host life may be lived in prisons: in prisons of war, in internment camps, in almshouses, hospitals, workhouses; by blind people, mental patients; in people who have to be wheeled about, washed, dressed and undressed by others; who are literally obliged to offer themselves to God in the hands of other people, like the Host in the priest's hands at the Mass.

A short time ago the *Daily Mirror* published a photograph of a baby in swaddling bands, tied by them on to a cruciform splint. It was to show a new hospital treatment, but to thousands it must have shown the crucified

Infant Christ. It was a little Host baby, redeeming the sins of the world in the Passion of innocence.

"*Agnus Dei, qui tollis peccata mundi: Dona nobis pacem.*"

It is more in frailty than in strength that Christ reveals Himself upon earth; more in littleness than in greatness; more in lowliness than in glory; for He is the Way and such is the Way of Love.

Christ said: "It is expedient to you that I go."

It is expedient, indeed. For nothing else but His going breaks the hard crust of our complacency and forces us to go out from ourselves to seek Him.

This seeking warms charity into life. It is not possible, if we have understood what is meant by Christ's abiding in man, to be shocked or narrow or hard again.

We understand what is meant by not pulling up the cockle lest we destroy the good grain. And the complexity and diversity of the needs that Christ wishes to experience in men make us realize why it is that He uses such strange material for His purpose; why it is that lives which, judged by our standards, are tragic and frustrated may, in fact, be the most glorious.

In this searching we become integrated ourselves. It gathers us together and makes us whole.

We are saved from the worst of all diseases—being satisfied. (To be at peace is a very different thing.) The man who is satisfied with himself and with things as they are to-day really admits despair.

Nothing can any longer be ugly to us in the sense of being repellent, for in this search we realize that God is everywhere, and everything reminds us of Him.

Before this longing, this desire, took hold of us, life was rather like a popular song, a little vulgar, a little absurd. But when we are in love, a popular song is informed with a totally different meaning. We associate it with the one we love, and its melody becomes enchanting.

It is impossible to know God, even through the sense of absence, without falling in love with Him, and when one is in love with God, life does become like a popular song which haunts us. Life as we have made it is indeed as cheap and tawdry as any popular song, but just because we now must be reminded of the beloved by every line of it and every note of it, it has become pure music and exquisite poetry for us.

By a curious paradox, our loss reveals the Divine Presence to us: Love is infinite desire.

On all the works of man we find the touch of Christ, provided that we are looking for some sign that God has been there. Even on the mass-produced goods that shame us, there is the sign. Each one of the millions is marked invisibly with a drop of blood from the stigmata. "Hands," we call the workers, forgetting that they are men and women. And "hands" they are, the hands that sin has nailed to the Cross of modern industry.

The works that have really grown from the loving work of men, from mind and heart and hands, work into which a man's own life has passed, give not only that man's life to the world for ever but one more visible sign to man of his image and likeness to God.

Even when the makers worked unconscious of their Divine prerogative, they were unconsciously imitating God; and therefore those who seek the lost Lord will find traces of His being and beauty in all that men have made, from music and poetry and sculpture to the gingerbread men in the *pâtisseries;* from the final calculation of the pure mathematician to the first delighted chalk drawing of a small child.

Only complacency can take away the sharp edge of love; boredom cannot do it and neither can aridity, for love is known as desire, which is stronger than we are and drives us as the wind drives a sail.

It is expedient that Christ should go, because we shall then seek, and seeking, touch the edge of the truths we cannot yet bear; because in the search we become aware of the wonder and mystery that contentment blinds us to.

Those who seek are more aware than any others. They observe every face; they look deep into every personality; they hear every modulation in the voice. They hear music and words and the sound of machinery, laughter and tears, with new hearing, attentive ears. They hear and see and taste life in a new way, with a finer consciousness, more analytically, because they are searching, because truth and only truth can ease their thirst; and with incomparably more delight, because, in this seeking, searching and finding are one thing: everywhere and in everyone they find what they seek.

But the finding is never complete. We can never know God exhaustively or completely; and in this life we cannot know even with the vision of the saints in heaven. But we can sometimes know with knowledge akin to the knowledge of the dead, for sometimes we become so aware of the fierce beauty of God's light that it seems to be known because it is burning within us.

This is very like Purgatory, and it is a pain which we would not willingly forgo once it has touched us, because it is our necessity and our joy. For Purgatory, after all, is the fire of the love of God, cauterizing the wound of sin.

Not everyone has the taste of Purgatory; but to all, Christ is still the Pied Piper who first enchanted and disturbed the house of the newly wakened soul with His enchanting music. Some of us, most of us, are like the lame boy who was left behind when the other children danced away with the Piper—but the lame boy still heard the music in his heart and still followed.

However lame our following, all is well, for the path is picked out by the impress of the Child's feet in the dust, and our seeking is, in itself, finding, a continual endorsement of the promise "Seek and ye shall find."

While we are seeking in one another for the lost Child, Our Lady still seeks and finds Him in us.

The gentleness that floods our hearts when we see a woman with child floods Our Lady's heart when she looks down upon the world, for through her the Holy Spirit has made humanity large with the Christ-child, and she, who is so essentially ours, who is one of the human race, is compelled with is in the mutual tenderness which can have but one answer: "Little children, love one another."

The Christhood that she recognizes in us is that we are her children: "Mother, behold your child."

This is the most wonderful trust of all, which Christ has given to us, to be Himself to Our Lady. He has actually given *His* love for her into our keeping. We are trustees of His love in our love for one another; He has given us His heart to give to the Bride of Life.

Devotion to Our Lady is the treasure of the Catholic Church. If proof were wanting that she is Christ's church, none could be surer than this. She has never ceased, all through the ages of Christianity, to foster this tender love for the Mother of God. As soon as a child can walk, he walks to Our Lady's altar and puts one more candle to shine among the countless candles at her feet, one more bunch of flowers from the fields is pushed into her hand or laid across her gilded shoes; and when he is old and nodding before the altar, it is the same thing.

Every trifling thing is told to her and every great sorrow; she is the sharer of all earth's joys and griefs.

She is not wearied with our littleness; her smile comes down to us like a benediction through the sea of flickering candles, and she blesses our wild flowers withering at her feet. For each one of us is "another Christ"; each one, to Mary, is her only child. It is therefore not tedious to her to hear the trifles that we tell her, to look at the bruises that we bring to her, and seeing our wound of sin, to heal it.

IN 1940

YES, I have always come to the crucifix to pray,
But I never knew Jesus Christ and His love until to-day,
I sought by the feeble ray of the dim light of my mind;
But now it is dark, I learn by touch as they do who are
  blind.
I feel the pulse of infinite love beat feebly like my own,
And the heart of God confined in space to a little cage of
  bone.

I have often pondered this but have never understood
How hands which heal are stark and still, nailed to a
  piece of wood.
The love that makes, the love that mends, my own weak
  Faith could guess,
But not the love that wills to bear man's utter helpless-
  ness,
The love in the womb, the love in the Host, the love in
  the burial bands,
The power and the gentleness of the love nailed fast by
  feet and hands.

I knew the common soil enclosed the Rood's strong root;
That therefore Christ remained with us, its Seed and
  Flower and Fruit.
But I did not know the last extreme of the mystery of
  love:
That when man is rent, on his fluttered breath of death
  descends the Dove.
The Dove descends and the seed is sown on the sigh of
  the last drawn breath.
And life smiles back through the hard grey dust of the
  frozen face of death.

THE ASSUMPTION

" In a dark night,
   with anxious love inflamed,
   O, happy lot !
   Forth unobserved I went,
   My house being now at rest."
         (THE DARK NIGHT OF
         THE SOUL—ST. JOHN
         OF THE CROSS)

" Rejoice with me,
   all ye who love me; for the most High hath
   chosen my heart, to set his throne therein,
   and the kingdom of the Son of his love."
         (OFFERTORY OF THE MASS,
         ON THE FEAST OF THE MOST
         HOLY HEART OF MARY)

I WAS told the story of an old Bavarian peasant woman.

When she was younger she lost her only son, and only child. He was killed in the last war. Her neighbours, remembering that she had almost idolized the child, thought that she would be inconsolable, and they were astonished when she adopted another son. They were still more astonished because he was a little Negro.

Her own son had been very fair, with straight, blond hair and light blue eyes; the child she now had, had a black, velvety face like a dark pansy, dark eyes, and curly hair.

She gave him everything that her son had owned. There was no doubt of her love for him. There could be none for those who saw her face, weather-beaten and lined, marked and sealed with sorrow, and yet shining with quiet happiness.

One day a neighbour said to her:

"I would never have thought that you would put another boy in your son's place."

"I have not," she answered, simply: "There is only one boy, Jesus Christ."

That woman knew blessedness which would not be possible to human nature had not Our Lady, whom she resembled so vividly, made it possible.

After the war there will be many thousands of women who will need to live as Our Lady did after the crucifixion.

A generation of mothers will need to know, with the heart, that "there is only one boy, Jesus Christ."

The world's future will depend upon this, upon everyone's realizing that the survival of all that is worth the cost of a man's blood depends upon how we foster the Christ-life in the souls of the children, and not only in the children, but in all the reborn of any age.

And not only the world's future, but our going to heaven, will depend on it.

All we know about Our Lady's life after the Crucifixion, is that the disciple John took her to live with him.

"From that hour that disciple took her into his own home."

There, in secrecy again, she lived what is certainly our life of preparation for heaven; in secrecy, but known to all those around her, as every Christian is.

In the first Advent, she had prepared to look upon the face of her Son by working for Joseph: cooking, cleaning, weaving, mending for him, and undoubtedly being a companion to him in thought, too.

Now she had come to another Advent, a preparation for seeing her Son's face in heaven, and it was to be lived out in exactly the same way.

We might have thought that even if she had not been allowed to go away to some place of solitude, to prepare for the birth of God by prayer and retirement, at least she might do so now, for now she was beginning to grow old. She had seen her Son through His life and death; she had closed His eyes and put Him into the tomb; and she must wait, to see those eyes opening again, until she got to heaven.

Now, at all events, she might have gone away, and

shutting out the distractions of the world, have folded her being upon the thought of God and waited His summons, rapt in contemplation.

But the opposite was her way.

Perhaps Our Lord took so young an apostle as John into His motley little company in order that he should be still a boy when he took Our Lady home. Perhaps, too, His very special love for John may have had something to do with the future, in which Christ foresaw John giving His Mother no time to grieve.

She had been crucified we know; and her longing for Christ is beyond our knowing; but faith and a boy in the house could make life very full. It is moving to think of her once more baking the kind of cakes she knew boys like; once more patching and darning, and sewing buckles on sandals; once more talking of the things that interested the boy and being a companion to his thought. And how fitting it was that the companion of John's thought should be Our Lady. For John's was the mind of crystal in which all the fires of love reflected, and Mary's was the mind of the girl who sang the Magnificat.

At length she died.

For us, death will be another First Communion—we simply cannot imagine what it was for the Bride of the Spirit.

We know that her body was taken to heaven, for God would not let corruption touch the flesh from which Christ's body was made.

But these things dazzle us and leave us stammering when we would like to sing.

No wonder that the most astonishing sermons are preached about Our Lady's Assumption.

They sometimes puzzle converts when they first hear them, for they seem to be descriptions by eye witnesses, and it is difficult to know how literally they are to be taken.

To the Catholic from the cradle they are not puzzling. He went to church before he could walk, and he lives with too little wonder in the midst of miracles. He knows that the descriptions the preacher gives are no more and no less than the "Holy Cards" which he used to eat during Benediction, when he was that solemn, unshakable creature, a Catholic baby.

They are better than the Holy Cards though, for each one of these sermons comes from a heart burning with a child's faith and truth that cannot be told.

They are in the great picture-book of the Church, illuminated pages, crudely drawn by a child, but drawn by a child whose mother has given him sanguine, vermilion, azure, and gold.

They say that when her time came to die, Our Lady was borne up to heaven in the hands of angels, borne through a blue sky that was warm with the noonday heat and yet was pale beside the blueness of her mantle.

The legions of saints waited her coming, glorious in garments scarlet and white, with burning haloes; and before them all came Gabriel, his mantle dazzling silver in the sunlight. Bowing low, he gave her a lily for a sceptre.

She passed the multitude of the angels and saints and came at last to a place of solitude; and here her Son came to her; and He was a king in a robe of rose, and His wounds were jewels that shone; and He crowned her with a great crown set with seven brilliant stars for her life's seven sorrows.

What does this all really mean?

Because we cannot conceive of heaven we have, in our own minds, almost whittled it away to nothingness. Because it is not a place as we understand place, we unconsciously think of it as nowhereness. In our dread of forming a materialist conception of it, we have conceived of it as nothing.

We do not know where or what or how heaven is, but this we know, and it is very nearly all that we know about heaven.

In heaven Our Lady is with God.

Our Lady's body is there, and the Body of Christ is there: and Our Lady's soul and the soul of Christ and His divinity.

We can realize this only in so far as we realize it through its effect upon the world.

There, before God, is humanity, our humanity; but innocent humanity in all its primal loveliness; humanity with which the Spirit of God is in love.

And she is ours !

Therefore, it is always Advent, always spring: The life and birth and death and resurrection of Christ always goes on upon earth, an unending circle of light.

Because even now, and always, the *fiat* is uttered, and the Love of the Spirit of Life is consummated in the Child Bride; the earth is continually made new; we are continually born again.

This is what really matters most of all to everyone: the power to be made new.

Not simply beginning again, dragging along with the old scars, the old crippling wounds, the old weakness dragging at the will; limping with the weariness of yesterday, sore with the heartsickness of the last defeat, bitter with the still smarting grievance against one another.

Not that, but real newness, being born again.

A new will, new heart, new vision, new love—indeed, new life.

Even in natural things, it is newness that gives us most delight: daybreak, morning in spring. These seem to us like promises from heaven, promises of our own renewal.

"I will give you the morning star."

To be born again: that is exactly what Christ has promised to us; not only once, but just as often as our inner life grows old and jaded and dies.

But newness, flowering spring, shadowless morning, are not born of what is decaying, corrupt and fetid.

They are born only of virginity, virginity which *is* newness, virginity complete as fire and water.

The only virginity like that is the virginity of Our Lady; it is through this virginity that the earth is made new, that the Holy Spirit is wed to humanity.

Through Mary of Nazareth Christ is born again and again in the individual heart.

"Blessed is the fruit of thy womb, Jesus," the little children say. And they do not understand what they say. But as they grow older, with the angel's prayer in their hearts, they begin to understand that this "fruit" is the Life of Christ born again in the world—always, everywhere.

Our Lady is in heaven.

On earth the breath of the spirit is stirring the young green corn. The song of the shepherd is heard in lambing time.

In heaven the music of the Incarnation is uttered eternally in its first simplicity.

The Mother has found the lost Child.

The empty Chalice is brimming with wine.

The Reed is filled with infinite music.

The Divine Little Bird is in His nest.